J.M. BARRIE

J. M. BARRIE

The Magic behind
Peter Pan

Susan Bivin Aller

LERNER PUBLICATIONS COMPANY • MINNEAPOLIS

For my boys
Bob, Hugh and Ben
who believed and clapped their hands

While only one person's name appears as author of this book, it took many other people to bring it to fruition. With gratitude for their encouragement, assistance, and critiques, the author wishes to thank the Simsbury Writers' Group, The Saturday Morning Club of Hartford, Joy Stafford, Barrie scholars Andrew Birkin and Karl Michael Emyrs, the Barrie Birthplace in Kirriemuir, and the staff of the Beinecke Rare Book and Manuscript Library at Yale University.

A toast and tribute, as well, to the skill and sensitivity of editor Susan Breckner Rose, and to the family and friends who have kept the vision alive!

Copyright © 1994 by Susan Bivin Aller

Library of Congress Cataloging-in-Publication Data

Aller, Susan Bivin.
    J. M. Barrie : the magic behind Peter Pan / Susan Bivin Aller.
       p.   cm.
    Includes bibliographical references and index.
    ISBN 0-8225-4918-2
    1. Barrie, J. M. (James Matthew), 1860-1937—Juvenile literature.
2. Authors, Scottish—20th century—Biography—Juvenile literature.
3. Peter Pan (Fictitious character)—Juvenile literature.
[1. Barrie, J. M. (James Matthew), 1860-1937. 2. Authors, Scottish.
3. Peter Pan (Fictitious character)] I. Title.
PR4076.A55 1994
828'.91209—dc20
[B]   94-5452
                                          CIP
                                          AC

Manufactured in the United States of America

1 2 3 4 5 6 – I/JR – 99 98 97 96 95 94

Contents

Nina Boucicault was the first actress to play Peter Pan. The play opened in London on December 27, 1904, with Nina's brother, Dion, as the producer.

ONE

In the Thin Form of a Play

December 27, 1904

What was it that made us eventually give to the public in the thin form of a play that which had been woven for ourselves alone?*
—J. M. Barrie, *Peter Pan*

Peter Pan gasped as Tinker Bell fluttered down and came to rest on her tiny bed.

"Why, Tink, you have drunk my medicine! It was poisoned and you drank it to save my life! Tink, dear Tink, are you dying?"

Peter Pan threw his arms out toward the audience and cried for them to save Tink. "Do you believe in fairies? Say quick that you believe! If you believe, clap your hands!"

Thunderous applause filled the theater, and the actress playing Peter Pan was so startled she burst into tears.

It was December 27, 1904—opening night for J. M. Barrie's new play, *Peter Pan: Or the Boy Who Would Not Grow Up.*

A short while before, festive crowds of theatergoers had milled about in front of the Duke of York's Theatre in London.

---

*The sources for the quotations in this book are on pages 122–124.

It was a foggy night, and women tucked their hands deep inside fur muffs while their escorts held on to their top hats. Horse-drawn cabs turned up the street from Trafalgar Square and formed a waiting line in St. Martin's Lane.

Rumors were circulating about this new play by the popular writer J. M. Barrie. One was about a dog's costume that had cost a small fortune to make. Barrie had sworn all the actors and stagehands to secrecy, and very few people could even find out what the new play was about.

All they knew was the title. *Peter Pan*. How curious. Was it a child's play? Or maybe a pantomime for adults?

When the doors opened, the people moved gratefully from the damp night into the theater's cream and gold interior, with its modern electric lighting and long corridors lined with portraits of famous actresses.

Behind the russet curtains of his private box, the playwright sat nervously smoking a pipe and pulling his muffler closer around his throat. Days of raw, misty weather had given him another miserable cold, and he was beginning to cough again. James Matthew Barrie was a small man—just over five feet tall—and his fine head, with its strong profile and expressive, deeply set blue eyes, seemed too dramatic for his stature. A dark, drooping mustache covered the sensitive mouth that rarely smiled. Even though he had lived in London for 20 years, nearly half his life, his deep voice still rumbled with the burred accent of his native Scotland. When he told a friend, "These *Peter Pan* rehearsals have given me a month's headache," it sounded as though he had said "haddock."

Tonight James was exhausted. He and the company of 50 actors had been up the previous night until dawn, trying to get every detail of the production just right. There were five elaborate sets, and music and dancing and flying equipment.

James Matthew Barrie at age 36

Some of it was still not ready. And nobody would ever see the magnificent scene he had written where an eagle swoops out over the audience, grabs Captain Hook, and drops him to the crocodile. It simply was too much for the stage crew to engineer.

James also worried about what the theater critics would write, and there were many of them in the audience tonight. He had great confidence in the director and the talented actors who had been rehearsing for weeks, but nothing like *Peter Pan* had ever been tried before. The first producer he showed the script to was sure Barrie had lost his mind, and he told a few people so. The producer who had finally decided to risk paying for the production was his American friend Charles Frohman. Frohman was also waiting anxiously tonight—on the other side of the Atlantic—wondering if he would lose the vast sums of money he had invested.

And what about Arthur and Sylvia Llewelyn Davies and their five boys? Why on earth had James put their games onto this stage? Would Arthur and Sylvia assume he was just trying to cash in on their friendship?

But James was an experienced playwright, and his instincts told him this was good material for the theater, very good. Later he would say that he could not remember actually writing it. *Peter Pan* was his dream child, made by rubbing the five Davies boys "violently together, as savages with two sticks produce a flame. That is all he is, the spark I got from you." But he knew there was so much more.

At 7:45 the orchestra began to play the overture, and the front curtain rose to reveal a dolls' house painted on a drop cloth. A large black-and-white dog walked onstage, knocked three times on the door, then went into the dolls' house. As the overture ended, a little housemaid came out, stamped her foot to get the conductor's attention, and then signaled him to begin the opening music.

As she made a smiling exit, the main curtain rose.

For a moment the audience was silent, trying to see what was onstage. Then they gasped in astonishment. The large dog was turning back the bedclothes in a night nursery. She ambled offstage and returned with a small boy riding on her back. "I won't go to bed, I won't, I won't!" he shouted.

A few minutes later the audience drew in its breath as Peter Pan crept through the window and darted around the nursery hunting for his shadow. The audience knew they were not watching a traditional Christmas pantomime, with its well-known fairy-tale plot and characters. The setting was familiar, for of course the audience recognized an English nursery. But some very unusual things were going on in this one. Who but a theatrical genius could have created a dog nursemaid and a ticking crocodile and a saucy fairy that was nothing more than a little flickering light? Who but James Barrie could have combined pirates, Indians, mermaids, and flying children into one magical performance?

Peter Pan has been flying from stages all over the world for nearly a century.

The audience joyfully followed the actors to Never Land, and as the curtain fell on the heartbreaking sight of Peter Pan looking wistfully into the nursery window, a roar went up. Curtain call followed curtain call. Three hours of magic had ended, and a theatrical legend had begun.

That night a telegram hummed across the wires to Charles Frohman, the producer waiting in New York: "Peter Pan all right. Looks like big success." Frohman was ecstatic.

James returned to see the play again and again during its original three-month run. He continually made changes in the script, until the prompter's copy was a mass of corrections. James delighted in taking children of friends backstage to show them how the mechanical tricks worked. Once he even put on the flying harness himself and whirled through the air.

Margaret Ogilvy with her first three children—Mary, Jane Ann, and Alexander. By the time Jamie was born—her ninth—he was thought of as just another mouth to feed.

❦ TWO ❦

To Be Born
1860–1866

To be born is to be wrecked on an island.
— J. M. Barrie, preface to *Coral Island*

"On the day I was born we bought six hair-bottomed chairs," James Barrie reported about his birthday.

The date was May 9, 1860, and the place was the small highland town of Kirriemuir, County Angus, Scotland. James Matthew Barrie first saw the world from an upstairs room in the stone house where his eight brothers and sisters had also been born. He was named James for his paternal grandfather and Matthew for the midwife, Nanny Matthew, who assisted at his birth and had "cradled all the Barries."

The baby was just another mouth to feed. But the chairs! "How they had been laboured for," James wrote. "In our little house it was an event.... Neighbours came in to see the boy and the chairs."

Jamie loved the little red town he called Kirrie. It had narrow streets that wound steeply between the houses made of the local reddish pink stone. Roads led away toward the rolling Sidlaw Hills and Dundee 17 miles to the south, and north toward the Grampian Mountains.

The house in which the Barrie family lived was a two-story stone house on the Brechin Road, connected to several other houses in a row called the Tenements. On the street in front, wagons rumbled by and handloom weavers pushed their wobs— finished bolts of cloth—in creaking barrows. The door and four windows on the back faced a yard and a stone wash house that were used by all the families in the Tenements.

Jamie's father, David, was a handloom weaver like most of the other homeowners in Kirriemuir. His loom nearly filled one downstairs room, and its click and whir were echoed by those of hundreds of other looms in the town. The neighbors

Jamie was born in an upstairs room in this stone house in Kirriemuir, Scotland. The small wash house is at left.

David Barrie and
Margaret Ogilvy

respected him for his honesty and genial ways. He didn't have much formal education, but he loved to read. He spent many hours studying the books of his favorite writers: Thomas Carlyle, William Gladstone, John Bunyan, and Edward Gibbon. His driving ambition was to see that his three sons got a college education, no matter what the cost to the rest of the family.

Jamie's mother was called by her family name, Margaret Ogilvy, as was the custom. She was a small, neat person who skillfully managed her house and large family. She had a strong personality and usually got her own way, but she saw the funny side of most things and would often double up with laughter. Her cooking and sewing skills were admired by many—especially young brides who came to learn from her. She had been reared in the strict Auld Licht, or Old Light, community of churchgoers. When she married David Barrie, she joined the Free Church where he belonged. But her childhood among the old-fashioned believers supplied her with many stories to tell her own children.

By the time Jamie was born, his oldest brother, Alexander, was already an outstanding scholar. Alexander was 18 years old and away studying at Aberdeen University. Jamie's 16-year-old sister Mary taught school near Kirriemuir. Jane Ann was 13, and although she had been to school, she spent much of her time helping their mother with the house and younger children.

The most promising of all the Barrie children was David. He was seven when Jamie was born. It was clear that David was their mother's favorite. He was a handsome, fun-loving boy who would become a minister in the church if she could have her way.

Two little girls, Sara and Isabella, were six and three when Jamie was born. And when Jamie was three, the last child, a girl named Margaret, joined the family. Two other Barrie children had died in infancy before Jamie was born.

When Jamie was six, his big brother David went away to a private school in Bothwell operated by their oldest brother Alexander. One night a telegram came from Alexander. Their father read the terrible news aloud: David had been ice skating when another boy accidentally knocked him down. He was in critical condition with a fractured skull and was not expected to live. It was the eve of his 14th birthday.

At once Margaret Ogilvy prepared to go to Bothwell "to get between Death and her boy." The family walked down to the train station with her, but as they waited, a second telegram arrived. "He's gone!" their father said huskily.

"Then we turned very quietly and went home again up the little brae."

Margaret Ogilvy was beside herself with grief. She lay for days in her bed weeping and calling out David's name as she held the christening dress that all her children had worn. Life went on as best it could for the rest of the family, and Jane Ann, now 20, took charge of the house.

Jamie was a quiet child and small for his age. He was deeply affected by his mother's behavior. He understood that David was dead. He and his little sister Margaret had played quietly under the draped table where David's coffin lay in their house. But even after the coffin was buried in the cemetery on the hill above the town, his mother would still not come out of her room.

He loved his mother and missed her company. He sat outside her door and began to cry.

Jane Ann found him there and urged him to go to his mother "and say to her that she still had another boy."

Cautiously, Jamie opened the door and peered in.

"Is that you?" called Margaret Ogilvy.

Jamie guessed that she thought David had come back, so he said sadly, "No, it's no him, it's just me."

At that, his mother called to him by name and cradled him in her arms. The long period of healing had begun for Margaret Ogilvy, and Jamie was to play an important role in it. It was his introduction to theater.

At the age of eight, Jamie wore a velveteen suit and a serious expression for his first photograph. He was in Glasgow, living with his older brother and sister and attending Glasgow Academy.

THREE

We Are Twelve

1866–1873

Nothing that happens after we are twelve matters very much.
— J. M. Barrie, *Margaret Ogilvy*

Jamie felt that if his brother David returned, his mother would be happy again. So he pretended to be David. He put on his brother's clothes and imitated his special whistle. At first his mother must have wept when he did this, but gradually she began to see the humor in it and occasionally even laughed. In a notebook, Jamie kept track of the number of times she laughed in a day and reported the number to the doctor when he came to check on her.

He became a convincing actor. At home he tried anxiously to please and impress her. He did everything he could to divert her from thinking about her dead son.

Acting the part of another person soon became easy for him. Once Jamie exchanged clothes with a friend who was not allowed to play while wearing dark mourning clothes. While his friend played games with the others, Jamie sat solemnly on the sidelines wearing the black clothes and trying to cry.

19

Jamie and his friend Mills, son of the local bookseller, spent hours setting up a toy theater with puppets, which they animated from behind the curtains of a large bed.

With his friend Robb, he produced original plays in the wash house behind the Tenements. They charged the neighbor children an admission of pins, a marble, or a top—called preens, a bool, and a peerie in the old Scots dialect. The thrilling climax of the drama came when the two performers tried to stuff each other into the wash boiler. Jamie and Robb would also sneak away from their parents to watch performances by traveling players, acrobats, and magicians who toured the Scottish countryside.

At about this time, the Barries sent Jamie to a local school owned by two young ladies. He called it the hanky school because the pupils were required to bring clean handkerchiefs every day—not for their noses, but to kneel on for prayers.

When he was eight, Jamie went away to Glasgow to live with his brother Alexander and, for the next three years, attended the academy where Alexander was teaching. Their sister Mary kept house for them.

While he was gone, the Industrial Revolution arrived in Kirriemuir. A linen factory with steam-powered machinery was built in the town where only handlooms had been used before. The town was jarred awake every morning at 5:30 by a blast from the factory whistle. The mill owners, needing cheap labor to run the machines, hired the women and girls of the town. Their husbands and fathers, who had owned and operated their handlooms at home, could not compete with the cheaper, faster power looms, so many men sat idle while the women went to the factories.

David Barrie was in his mid-50s, but he knew that he had to change with the times. In 1870, he applied for a job as a

At the local school in Forfar, 11-year-old Jamie was photographed with his class. He is in the front row at far left.

factory bookkeeper in Forfar, a town six miles from Kirriemuir. When he got the job, he moved his family there.

The next year Alexander was transferred to another district. So Jamie, at the age of 11, had to return home to study, this time at the local school in Forfar. It was a memorable year—the year he discovered how stories could flow from his imagination through a pen onto paper.

Margaret Ogilvy loved to tell stories, and Jamie was an eager listener. As she recovered from her grief over the death of her son David, she began to tell Jamie stories about her childhood with her own brother David. Their mother had died when Margaret was just eight years old, and Margaret became housekeeper for her father and little brother.

Jamie and his mother read many stories together. Her favorite subject was biography—especially of "men who had

Jamie was an avid reader of Chatterbox *magazine.*

been good to their mothers." She shivered with delight when the newspapers reported the victorious return of an explorer from an expedition. But her first thought was about how the explorer's mother felt. "She's a proud woman this night," she would say.

Robinson Crusoe was the first book they read aloud to each other. Then they read it again. *"Arabian Nights* should have been the next, for we got it out of the library (a penny for three days), but on discovering that they were nights when we had paid for knights we sent that volume packing, and I have curled my lips at it ever since."

Jamie and his mother borrowed books and rented books, and once in awhile, he was allowed to buy a book at the shop owned by the father of his friend Mills. "While buying (it was the occupation of weeks) I read, standing at the counter, most of the other books in the shop, which is perhaps the most exquisite way of reading."

He subscribed to a magazine called *Sunshine,* and waited impatiently for it to arrive each month. In every issue was a continued story about "the dearest girl, who sold water-cress, which is a dainty not grown and I suppose never seen in my native town. This romantic little creature took such hold of my imagination that I cannot eat water-cress even now without emotion."

"Why should I not write the tales myself?" he asked himself one day. Or, more likely, Margaret Ogilvy suggested the idea to stop him from pestering her while she was doing housework. He went up to a room in the garret of the house, and soon the stories began to flow in a torrent from his pen.

> They were all tales of adventure...the scene lay in un-known parts, desert islands, enchanted gardens, with knights (none of your nights) on black chargers, and round the first corner a lady selling water-cress....
>
> From the day on which I first tasted blood in the garret my mind was made up; there could be no hum-dreadful-drum profession for me; literature was my game.

Within a year, David Barrie was promoted to principal clerk of the new linen factory in Kirriemuir, so the family went back to the little red town on the banks of the Gairie River. Only now the prospering Barries rented a much larger house.

But the magical time with his mother was over. Now Jamie was turning 13. His family sent him to Dumfries, where there was a fine academy and where he could again live with his brother Alexander and sister Mary.

Jamie was not at all sure he wanted to leave home.

"The horror of my boyhood was that I knew a time would come when I also must give up the games, and how it was to be done I saw not."

An illustration in Chatterbox *in 1872 showed boys playing pirates, much as Jamie and his schoolmates were doing at Dumfries Academy that year.*

FOUR

To Open Doors with His Pen

1873–1884

In a London fog...he may have to grope for key-holes until at last he finds one in which his key turns. So it often was with Anon trying to open doors with his pen.
— J. M. Barrie, *The Greenwood Hat*

Instead of giving up the games, Jamie found other boys at Dumfries Academy who loved playing out adventure stories as much as he did. They had all read the books of James Fenimore Cooper and Robert M. Ballantyne, and when they could escape from their studies, they met near the school where wooded grounds sloped down to a river.

It was there, "when the shades of night began to fall, certain young mathematicians shed their triangles, crept up walls and down trees, and became pirates." It was their joy to be "wrecked every Saturday for many months in a long-suffering garden."

Jamie knew that he had to work hard at Dumfries so he could qualify for a university. But his main interests were not academic. "We have been having some great discussions in the Debating Society," he wrote to a friend. "The Gaiety

A small Jamie Barrie (back row, far left) *is shown at the age of 14 with his Dumfries Academy class.*

Company from Glasgow are here just now. I was there on Friday seeing *As You Like It*. I liked it very much....I am going down to see Sanger's Circus in a little, so please excuse hasty writing."

He led the amateur dramatic club of the school in a production of his first play—in six scenes and fifteen minutes—

> a staggering work entitled *Bandelero the Bandit*. I was not Bandelero....because I thought one of the other parts was better. It was the part of all my favourite characters in fiction rolled into one, so that I had to be constantly changing my clothes, with the result that I was scarcely ever on stage.

A local clergyman wrote a letter to the Dumfries newspaper about *Bandelero the Bandit*. He criticized the school authorities for allowing "certain young men to befool themselves."

At 17 Jamie wrote his first play, Bandelero the Bandit, *for the Dumfries Amateur Dramatic Club. He also acted in all three plays on this program.*

Undaunted, Jamie wrote a three-volume novel while at Dumfries and boldly sent it to a publisher. The publisher wrote back with praise for the work and offered to print it if the author would pay him one hundred pounds.

Jamie was shorter than average, and that was probably one reason he did not try to play games that needed great size or strength. But he had endurance, built up by walking miles and miles. He wrote proudly to a friend about one marathon walk: "C. Wilson and I had a long walk a few Saturdays ago from Dumfries to Carlisle (33 miles in 9½ hrs.). It got into the papers under the head 'Plucky Pedestrians,' a name the Academy boys have taken up and given us."

Jamie kept a log of the mileage he walked during a summer holiday: "Walked *18* times. Average of 13$\frac{11}{18}$ in all *245* miles."

Margaret Ogilvy thought it was just showing off to walk "with no end save the good of your health." And she told him so. "Ay, Jeames, are you off for your walk?" she would ask with sarcasm in her voice, and then add, "Rather you than me!"

"She never 'went for a walk' in her life....and she never lost the belief that it was an absurdity introduced by a new generation with too much time on their hands."

James was not a particularly good student, but his family expected him to go to a university. He did not want to be a lawyer or a doctor; he wanted to write. So his understanding brother Alexander helped out by suggesting Edinburgh University, where James could study with some of the finest classical and literary scholars of the day. If literature was to be his game, it would be nurtured by these great professors in Edinburgh.

James actually did very well in his literature classes and won some minor academic prizes. After four years at Edinburgh, at age 22, he proudly put on his cap and gown, had his

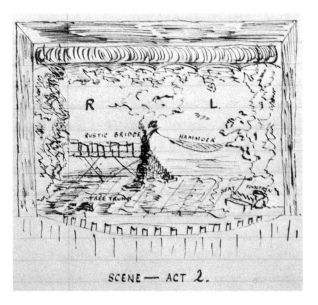

James's set design for a play he wrote at Edinburgh University

"J. M. Barrie, M.A." in his graduate's cap and gown at Edinburgh University, 1882

picture taken, and received his master's degree. Now he had to prove to his family that he could make a living with his pen. After a summer at home, he returned to Edinburgh to give his new profession a try. There could be no frivolous three-volume novels or *Bandelero the Bandit* now. This time he would write a scholarly treatise, "The Early Satirical Poetry of Great Britain." Meanwhile, he tried to support himself by writing theater and book reviews for the local paper.

But at Christmastime, with very little to show of his literary project, he moved back home to Kirriemuir. Jane Ann—his sister who was still at home caring for their parents and the house—found a want ad for a newspaper leader writer in the English city of Nottingham. The job required someone who could write five leaders, or feature articles, a week. And it paid quite well.

> It suddenly struck me that the leaders were the one
> thing I had always skipped. Leaders! How were they writ-
> ten? . . . . I retired to ponder, and presently she [Margaret
> Ogilvy] came to me with the daily paper. Which were the
> leaders? she wanted to know, so evidently I could get no
> help from her. Had she any more newspapers? I asked,
> and after rummaging, she produced a few with which her
> boxes had been lined. Others, very dusty, came from
> beneath carpets, and lastly a sooty bundle was dragged
> down the chimney. Surrounded by these I sat down, and
> studied how to become a journalist.

Jane Ann urged him to apply and suggested that he ask one of his university professors for a reference. The newspaper asked for a sample of his writing, and he sent them a school essay on *King Lear.* James was more surprised than anyone when he was offered the position. But he was uneasy about going far away to Nottingham and giving up his freedom by taking a job, even though it paid a princely salary of three pounds a week.

During the year and a half he spent in Nottingham, James learned how to write regularly on a great variety of topics. The paper needed someone who could fill up columns of newsprint—it didn't matter what the subjects were. James was certainly well suited for the job. His imagination soared over a wide range of topics he often knew little or nothing about. Articles poured from his pen and were printed under such headlines as "Mothers-in-Law," "Male Nursery Maids," and "Parasites." With constant practice, his skill at observing and recording life developed. With the same constant practice, his handwriting deteriorated into a scrawl that was almost unreadable.

One thing bothered James, however. He never saw his own name in print because all his articles were published anonymously or under a pseudonym thought up by the newspaper. He referred to himself during these and his early London years as "James Anon."

Now James began to catch a larger vision of what the literary game could be for him. He started sending articles to more important newspapers and journals in London, and with growing frequency—to his triumph—some were purchased for publication.

Then a new idea struck him.

> Nearly eighteen months elapsed before there came to me, as unlooked for as a telegram, the thought that there was something quaint about my native place. A boy who found that a knife had been put into his pocket in the night could not have been more surprised.

He wrote an article called "An Auld Licht Community," based on his mother's childhood memories, and the influential editor Frederick Greenwood bought it for London's *St. James Gazette*. James proudly sent a copy of it home to his mother in Kirriemuir.

"When she read that first article she became alarmed, and fearing the talk of the town, hid the paper from all eyes," in a bandbox on the garret stairs, reported James. But after James sold several more of the Auld Licht articles, she asked him if he was paid for them just as he was for the others. "When she heard that I was paid better, she laughed again and had them out of the bandbox for re-reading, and it cannot be denied that she thought the London editor a fine fellow but slightly soft."

When the Nottingham paper found it could buy syndicated articles for less money than they were paying James, they cut out his job. He returned, unemployed and somewhat deflated, to Kirriemuir. But he continued to bombard London editors

Some characters from Auld Licht Idylls *as drawn by William Hole*

with his articles. His mother and sister helped think up subjects to write about and celebrated whenever he sold one.

He soon came to believe that he could earn his living as a freelance journalist in London. Greenwood had written, "But I liked that Scotch thing—any more of those?" So James sent him an article about the rooks building nests in Dumfries and added a note asking if he should come to London and work as a writer.

Greenwood, who had received many such requests from eager young men, replied no.

"So I went."

Packing his clothes, notebooks, *Roget's Thesaurus,* and a folding desk into a trunk, James took the night train to London. He was 24. He carried his money in a secret pocket, which he checked from time to time. He was armed with his mother's warnings about London, "to walk in the middle of the street (they jump out on you as you are turning a corner), never to venture forth after sunset, and always to lock up everything." London, which she had read about but had never seen, was "a monster that licked up country youths as they stepped from the train."

When James got off the train at St. Pancras Station in London the next morning, he spotted an advertisement for the *St. James Gazette.* Listed in the table of contents was "The Rooks Begin to Build." By Anon, of course. But he knew it was the article he had sent to Greenwood only a few days before.

James later wrote about himself as the young man who had just arrived by train:

> In other dazzling words, having been a minute or so in London, he had made two guineas. This may not seem a great thrill to you, but try it in his circumstances. I remember how he sat on his box and gazed at this glorious news about the rooks....It was almost as if Greenwood had met me at the station.

James loved the hard work of writing. Here he is seen working during a visit to his parents' home in 1890. One of the hair-bottomed chairs, bought on the day of his birth, is at right.

In Love with Hard Work
1884–1890

I fell in love with hard work one fine May morning.
— J. M. Barrie, *M'Connachie and J. M. B.*

James knew London only in his imagination. He and his mother had often pretended to take trips to London in which they ate in fine restaurants and winked to his books in shop windows. Such was his confidence that he would become a successful writer.

Of these fantasies, James said that he and his mother

> were most gleeful...calling at publishers' offices for a cheque... "Will you take care of it, or shall I?" I asked gaily, and she would be certain to reply, "I'm thinking we'd better take it to the bank and get the money," for she always felt surer of money than of cheques, so to the bank we went ("Two tens, and the rest in gold"), and thence straightway (by cab) to the place where you buy sealskin coats for middling old ladies....
>
> "If you could only be sure of as much as would keep body and soul together," my mother would say with a sigh.

"With something over, mother, to send to you."
"You couldna expect that at the start."

Now the fantasy was over and James was truly in London.

He sat for some time on his trunk, gazing at the advertisement for the *St. James Gazette*. Then he bought a copy of the paper itself and "breakfasted triumphantly, on what I forget, but we may be sure it was chiefly on rooks."

"Coat buttoned against burglars," as his mother had cautioned, James found a rooming house and hauled his trunk upstairs to "a room not much larger than a piano case; it was merely the end of a passage, and was only able to call itself a room because it had a door. It looked on to a blank wall, two or three yards away, with a dank tree between him and the wall." He set up his folding desk and prepared for the literary life. "He also bought a penny bottle of ink to heave at the metropolis, and began the heaving before noon."

His darting pen covered page after page with articles intended for newspapers. He wrote at least two a day for several months. He didn't sell them all. In fact, he sent 14 articles to newspaper editors before he sold even one.

James was very thrifty. Most days his food consisted of four halfpenny buns, which he ate with jam and other delicacies sent him by his mother. She was sure his pen would run dry and he would starve. Sometimes he bought cheese or baked potatoes from a street vendor.

There were "some good old miserable times" in the early days when he watched for the postman to "drop our fate into the letter-box or heartlessly go by[.] It fell as soft as pound notes when it was a [printer's] proof, and like a damn when it was itself come back again." When most discouraged, he looked out his window at the tree and counted its leaves.

James had heard that a writer should not approach an editor without wearing a top hat. So he bought one to impress Greenwood. It never fit him very well, and it fell off if he stopped abruptly. But he wore it whenever he went to see an editor. Sometimes he even wore it when he was writing, in the hopes that it would bring him luck.

Whether it was luck or hard work, he began to sell more articles. Within a year of arriving in London, James had nearly achieved his goal of earning a pound a day by his writing. Any subject would do for an article. If he couldn't find something interesting on his walks or from his memories of Scotland, he would pretend to be someone else. It was a grownup version of the same game he played as a boy, and it was still fun.

> My experiences as a medical man—I can still smell the dispensary I was never in; I have been a member of the House of Commons...I was vagrants of all sorts, and as many men of property...There was a fascinating series... about my life as a civil engineer in India, where I threw a bridge across the Irrawaddy. I forget how many thousand coolies I employed, but even now I can look over your heads and see rickshaws being trotted across the bridge I threw.

James called these "the soap-bubbles of Anon." Greenwood bought articles from a number of young, aspiring freelance writers, and he liked to refer to them as being written by Bob or Bill or Thomas Anon.

James Anon became very eager to see his own name in print. So he wrote a book. It was called *Better Dead* and was a macabre comedy about an organization that murdered people whose names appeared too often in the newspapers. When he couldn't find any publisher who would buy it, he paid for the printing himself. He was very proud of the book, and

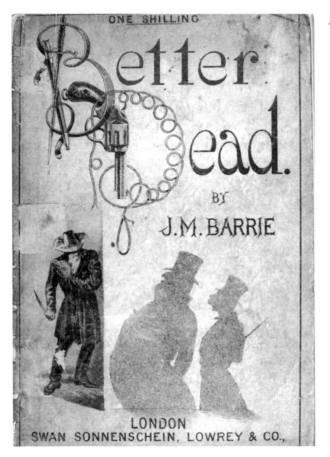

James paid a publisher to print his first book, a satire.

sometimes stood near newsstands hoping to see someone pay a shilling for it.

In 1888, when he had been in London just three years, James had his first real success as an author. He compiled 12 articles he had written about the Auld Licht people of his mother's childhood and sold them to the publishing company of Hodder and Stoughton.

Margaret Ogilvy was surely proud of her son when *Auld Licht Idylls* appeared, handsome in a blue cover with a gilt top edge and the name of J. M. Barrie stamped on the spine. The book sold so quickly that James and his publishers decided to take advantage of his popularity by putting out another book of collected essays. This was about his experiences working on the newspaper in Nottingham. They called it *When a Man's Single*. In the following year, another book of his Scottish stories appeared, *A Window in Thrums,* and it was also a bestseller.

But not everybody liked James's writing. The people in Kirriemuir felt he was making fun of their habits and religious beliefs, and it was many years before they forgave him.

By this time, James had made a lot of friends among writers and editors and was a member of two well-known London clubs, the Garrick and Savage. He was proud to be called one of Henley's young men, a group that gathered around William Ernest Henley, the respected editor of the *Scots Observer* and later of the *National Observer.* Henley had a personal magnetism that attracted many writers, and his circle included Rudyard Kipling, Thomas Hardy, and H. G. Wells. Robert Louis Stevenson had been part of the group before he moved to Samoa. When he heard that J. M. Barrie, a fellow Scot, had joined Henley's circle, Stevenson began a correspondence with James that continued until Stevenson's death.

Soon James was writing another book, this time a long novel called *The Little Minister.* It too was set in Scotland, but instead of being a collection of essays, it was a long romantic story about Babbie, a gypsy girl, and Gavin Dishart, a minister in a Scottish town. Sales of this book made James a rich man.

Seven years after moving to London, James could consider himself a success, but he was ambitious for more. He wrote almost compulsively for hours each day. "I fell in love with hard work one fine May morning," he said. "The most precious possession I ever had—my joy in hard work."

BARRIE'S SENTIMENTAL TOMMY IN SCRIBNER'S

James's early books were very popular in the United States, and in 1896 Scribner's *magazine published* Sentimental Tommy *in installments. Its main character is a boy who wants to be a writer but who doesn't want to grow up.*

SIX

Ever a Boy

1890–1895

Poor Tommy! he was still a boy, he was ever a boy, trying sometimes as now, to be a man, and always when he looked round he ran back to his boyhood as if he saw it holding out its arms to him and inviting him to come back and play.
—J. M. Barrie, *Tommy and Grizel*

The boy who had feared he must "give up the games," was now a man of 30. And he had found ways to continue the games. Once he referred to Robert Louis Stevenson as "the spirit of boyhood, tugging at the skirts of this old world of ours and compelling it to come back and play." This was true of James as well.

With the freedom of being a freelance writer, James could go to visit his friends or his family in Scotland whenever he wanted to. He especially enjoyed visiting the households with children. "Uncle Jim" was a favorite of his nieces and nephews, and he was also popular with the children of literary friends. Margaret Henley, the young daughter of the editor William Ernest Henley, was especially fascinated by him.

41

He had an extraordinary talent for drawing children to him without seeming to seek their attentions at all. Many of them were first attracted by his "famous manipulation of the eyebrows." He explained:

> I alone of boys had been able to elevate and lower my eyebrows separately; when one was climbing my fore-head the other descended it, like the two buckets in the well....It is an appeal to the intellect, as well as to the senses, and no one on earth can do it except myself.

He once walked into the woods with two small visitors and led them to a tree with a hollow trunk. Inside the hollow they found a peapod, and inside the peapod was a tiny folded letter. James told them a fairy had written it and that he could read it to them. The enchanted children found several more letters in peapods before their visit ended.

He liked to play cricket with older children. Cricket was always his favorite ball game as a boy, and he never outgrew his love for it. He organized a group of writers—including Arthur Conan Doyle and A. A. Milne—into a team that played weekend cricket matches against other amateurs. James's team was called the "Allahakbarries." A traveler who had just come from Morocco told them that "Allah Akbar" was the Arabic phrase for "Heaven help us," and it was only a short leap from that to a pun on Barrie's name.

In spite of his popularity with children and his love of playing games, James was not always a pleasant person to be near. All his life he suffered from what were probably migraine headaches, and when one of these struck him down he was miserable for days at a time. When he was writing, he did not like to have anyone disturb him. He also fell into long silences that embarrassed other people. Even close friends could suddenly be cut off with a surly grunt or cold stare, and they might never know what they did to deserve it.

He could be the life of the party when he chose to, but it was hard to tell whether he was joking or not because he rarely smiled. James explained this by saying that he was once awarded a prize for being the schoolboy with the sweetest smile, and that as a tragic result, "I lost my smile. I suppose it is still jiggling about somewhere in the void, but it has never come back to me." He repeated this story to many audiences over the years, and they never failed to respond with laughter—while James's face remained stony.

From the time he saw his first traveling actors in Scotland, he loved watching plays being performed. And he delighted in

A cartoon of "J. M. Barrie in a play-ful mood"

writing dialogue in his novels. "I would preach in dialogue if I were a clergyman, and write my prescriptions in it if I were a physician." As a result, he decided to try his hand at writing plays for the London stage.

The first two plays he wrote were *Richard Savage* and *Ibsen's Ghost*. Two friends, who were fellow members of the Garrick Club, were actors and producers looking for new plays, and they agreed to produce them on the London stage. The plays had fairly short runs, but their success was enough to kindle James's love of standing in the wings, tinkering with the script, and watching his magic unfold onstage. Gradually he shifted from writing novels to writing plays.

James thought he was fairly uninteresting to women, primarily because he was so short. "Why have you never tried a short hero?" he once demanded of a group of novelists. There were some pretty young actresses, however, who found the rich, successful writer to be quite attractive, and he enjoyed the attention they gave him.

Walker, London was James's third play. It was a slapstick comedy about a group of people spending a weekend on a houseboat. The second lead was played by a pretty and flirtatious 29-year-old actress named Mary Ansell.

Mary had invested money in a theater company and had been touring with it, hoping to be discovered and offered roles on the London stage. Her father, who was dead, had been a licensed victualer, or pub owner, in London. Her mother now ran a boarding house in a south coast resort town. Mary had not had a very secure family life or much schooling, but she was attractive and ambitious and was determined to have a career in the theater. A friend of James's had seen her onstage and suggested her for a role in his play. James met her, was delighted, and offered her the part.

Mary Ansell in
Walker, London

During the run of the play, James gradually realized that his feelings about Mary were different from those he had for other young women. She knew how to tease him out of the dark moods that made him so gloomy. She was intelligent and stylish. And she was as short as he was. He was happy when they were together, but he wasn't sure he wanted to be a married man.

For months James had been making notes for a new novel. He was beginning to create the character of Sentimental Tommy, a boy who grew to manhood but could not become an adult emotionally. Tommy remained a boy at heart—selfish, irresponsible, and in the end, tragic. Many passages in the book sound like a young man arguing with himself about whether or not he should marry.

James and Mary finally became engaged, but they tried to keep the news secret until James could go to Kirriemuir and tell his family. While he was there, he caught pneumonia, and Mary quickly went to be with him and help nurse him back to health. When he recovered, James and Mary were married in the Barries' home. Then they went to Switzerland for a long honeymoon.

James's wedding present to his wife was a St. Bernard puppy, bought in Switzerland and shipped to them when he was old enough to travel. They named the puppy Porthos, after the St. Bernard in a novel by George du Maurier. Mary wrote:

Porthos was bought by the Barries in Switzerland while they were on their honeymoon, and they treated him like their child.

"Porthos was a baby when I first saw him, a fat little round young thing....My heart burnt hot for love of him."

During the first years of their marriage, James and Mary lived in a red brick house at 133 Gloucester Road in London. It was not far from Kensington Gardens, and every afternoon they took Porthos for a walk in the gardens.

Mary, tiny and elegant in her stylish coat and hat, emerged from the house first. Then the great dog, his full tan and white coat shining from Mary's frequent grooming, padded out the door after her. James, short and slight, bundled in a long, over-sized coat with muffler and hat, came last. The huge, sad-eyed St. Bernard grew more animated as they neared the gardens and would jump up playfully on his master or mistress. He was as tall as they were when he stood on his hind legs.

Mary wrote:

> On the way, we called in at a certain toy shop to buy a toy for Porthos. 'What age child would the toy be for?' demanded the shop-lady. Such an embarrassing question, for there stood 'the child' eagerly eyeing them. But I couldn't let on, could I? He adored dolls, and things that wound up and ran round and round by themselves.

James would write for hours at his desk in an upstairs study, while Porthos lay on a sofa nearby, watching him with his mournful eyes. As soon as James was done for the day, they would begin to roughhouse. Mary loved to watch them play, but there were times when she held her breath.

> They had fearful wrestling matches. These went on until both were exhausted. And they ran races, in and out of rooms, up and down the stairs, out of the front door, in by the back, over and over again. Mats and rugs were scattered in every direction. When it was all over I went round collecting the debris.

James with his mother, Margaret Ogilvy, in 1893. She fired his ambition to become a famous author, and he responded by including her as a fictionalized character in almost everything he wrote.

SEVEN

For Her

1895-1896

*Everything I could do for her in this life I have done since
I was a boy; I look back through the years and I cannot
see the smallest thing left undone.*
— J. M. Barrie, *Margaret Ogilvy*

After the Barries had been married a year, they decided to go to Scotland again to visit James's family and then take a vacation in Switzerland. Margaret Ogilvy was 76 years old. She was very frail, and her mind wandered. But she still glowed with pride in her son. Jane Ann had been reading James's latest book to her, and when Margaret saw him she smiled playfully and said, "I'm thinking I am in it again!"

She and James had played this game for years: he would show her his newest book, and she would find herself in it—thinly disguised. Then she would point it out with delight, while he stoutly denied that it was true. She told him she was afraid there would be a public scandal if people found out how often and in how many guises she appeared in his books.

James and Mary had scarcely begun their holiday in Switzerland when a telegram arrived with the news that Jane

49

Ann had died. They were shocked. They had just received her daily letter in the morning mail and had no indication that she was even ill. No one had suspected that she was suffering from cancer until the morning when she was too weak to get out of bed. Twelve hours later she was dead.

James and Mary left Switzerland at once to return to Scotland. David Barrie and his other daughters had tried to break the news of Jane Ann's death to Margaret Ogilvy, but she didn't seem to understand.

It was a three-day journey by train and boat from Switzerland to London and then to Kirriemuir. By the time James and Mary arrived, Margaret Ogilvy, too, was dead.

On the day she died, they told James, she went into his old room and said, "The beautiful rows upon rows of books, and he said every one of them was mine, all mine!" And yet, near the end, she called out, "Is that you, David?" As proud as she was of her son James, she could not forget the other shining boy who never grew up.

James paid tribute to the mother he adored in a book called *Margaret Ogilvy, by her son J. M. Barrie*. It sold thousands of copies and was hailed by some as "an unmatched story of the divinest of human emotions, a mother's love." Others criticized it as pure sentimentality. Barrie, some said, "threw the portrait of his mother into the whirlpool of commerce: in cold fact, cashing in on his own popularity." Nevertheless, James had recorded his childhood, even though—as an artist and not a historian—it was probably a mixture of fact and fantasy.

Margaret Ogilvy, *James's tender tribute to his mother, appeared in 1896, a few months after her death. This engraving from the first edition was probably modeled on a photograph of Margaret.*

J. M. Barrie, a famous and successful author at age 36

EIGHT

A Grown-Up with Them

1896–1898

*The Gardens are a tremendous big place, with millions
and hundreds of trees....In the Broad Walk you meet all the
people who are worth knowing, and there is usually a grown-up
with them to prevent their going on the damp grass.*
— J. M. Barrie, *The Little White Bird*

In September 1896, James and Mary sailed for America. They were met by reporters, eager to interview the author of *A Window in Thrums* and *The Little Minister,* which were very popular with American readers. "It is a most enviable position that Mr. Barrie occupies in literature, and he has gained distinction at an early age, for he is only thirty-six," the *New York Times* gushed.

The Barries were poor sailors. They were still recovering from seasickness when they landed. Two days later, a large headline over the story read "Barrie's First Interview: The writer and his wife arrive, sick and tired."

The article went on to describe them:

> The author is scarcely 5 feet 4 inches in height, and weighs not more than 125 pounds. He has pale cheeks and a big head, crowned with bushy hair. His noticeable

Mary Ansell Barrie, at the time of her marriage

features are his forehead and nose, both prominent....He has a dark brown mustache, which almost conceals his mouth. He was dressed yesterday in a suit of mixed Scotch material not particularly new, and wore a blue overcoat with a velvet collar, much the worse for wear, and a black derby hat.

Mrs. Barrie is a handsome young woman of the English type, whose nationality would never be questioned by any one who saw her. She was enveloped in a mackintosh.

During their six-week visit, the Barries traveled from New York to Boston, south to New Orleans, back to Washington, D.C., and finally to Canada. Everywhere they went, they were honored by writers and publishers and theatrical people. James loved the attention, but he never got used to being hounded by the American press.

He had two reasons for visiting America. One was to arrange for U.S. copyrights of his works so that unauthorized editions of his novels could not be sold. The other was to meet Charles Frohman, the American theatrical producer, and talk about producing a dramatized version of *The Little Minister.*

Barrie's friend Charles Frohman, the American producer

American actress Maude Adams as Babbie in The Little Minister.

One night Frohman took the Barries to the theater to see the American actress Maude Adams. James was charmed by her, and at once he decided that she should play the lead role of Babbie in *The Little Minister.*

James was glad when the trip was over. He had missed his long, solitary hours of writing. He enjoyed being a celebrity in America, but the pace of traveling and meeting all those famous people was exhausting. Now he had a new project to work on, a sequel to *Sentimental Tommy* called *Tommy and Grizel.* In this book, Tommy is in love with a woman named Grizel. James often used his own experiences as a basis for his fiction, but he was finding this romance difficult to write.

Parts of the story came dangerously close to revealing too much about problems that were beginning to disturb his marriage.

There was another dilemma he needed to solve. When he began the story, he visualized Grizel as being like Mary; but as the work progressed, he found he couldn't quite make his perfect woman Grizel from the real-life Mary. He needed to find a new model for his heroine.

One day while walking Porthos in Kensington Gardens, James caught sight of three stalwart little boys with their nurse. They were handsome children, the eldest about five, the second a year or so younger, and the third still a baby in his pram. The two older ones were dressed in corduroy trousers, high laced boots, and red tam-o'-shanter caps.

The boys were probably curious about the little man with the huge dog. The man was old, the boys thought, but somehow he was not quite grown up. Sometimes he raced and wrestled with the dog instead of walking along like other grownups. He did the most amazing tricks with his eyebrows. And he could wiggle his ears!

As one golden day followed another in Kensington Gardens, James cast his spell over the two older boys, whose names, he learned, were George and Jack. He began to include them in his play with the gentle Porthos. Then the games became stories, told by James, which the boys acted out along with the dog and James himself. The stories continued from day to day. They became more exciting. Sometimes the man was cowardly and the boys bravely rescued him. Sometimes the dog was a wild animal they had to escape from. This was an easy trick for Porthos, who loved to play hide and seek. The games went on until the starchy nursemaid, pushing the pram with the baby Peter in it ahead of her, broke the spell and led her charges home for tea—and a good washing. She was not amused by this man. He undermined her attempts to discipline the boys.

On New Year's Eve, the last day of 1897, the Barries went to a party given by a distinguished society lawyer for 70 of his fashionable friends. James found himself seated next to a delightful woman named Sylvia. She was married to Arthur Llewelyn Davies, a young lawyer. James was not alone in thinking that she was the prettiest woman in the room. Her father was the late George du Maurier, the famous novelist and illustrator for *Punch* magazine, and her brother was Gerald du Maurier, the actor.

James was amused to see Sylvia putting after-dinner candies into her purse. She told him she was taking them home to Peter.

How old was Peter? James wanted to know.

Nearly a year, Sylvia told him. And she had two older boys: George was almost five and Jack nearly four.

James's heart surely leaped. Did they play in Kensington Gardens in the afternoons? And did they wear red tam-o'-shanters?

Sylvia must have laughed with pleasure. Here at last was the man with the big dog she'd heard so much about from her boys. What a delightful discovery. Her children's friend was none other than the famous author James Barrie.

It wasn't long before the Barries and the Davieses were seen together on other social occasions. And the afternoon games in Kensington Gardens went on. When the gardens closed for the day, James often walked with the boys to their house nearby. Sometimes he stayed on to continue the storytelling right up until their bedtime. Arthur Llewelyn Davies was not always happy to have James show up at his house unannounced.

The Davies boys filled much of James's leisure time, but writing still occupied most of his working hours. *Tommy and Grizel* was finally taking shape. It needed some revisions, however, because Grizel was beginning to look and act like Sylvia Llewelyn Davies rather than Mary. The enchanting Sylvia, with her crooked smile and gray eyes, seemed to be taking over more than just his pen.

And James was taking over Sylvia's boys, leading them on an adventure toward a place to which he alone knew the way: the Never Land.

Peter, George, and Jack Llewelyn Davies

James photographed the Davies boys as they played out the stories they created together. In this photo, James noted that Jack was "removing crocodiles."

NINE

A Different Story

1898–1901

The following is our way with a story: First, I tell it to him, and then he tells it to me, the understanding being that it is quite a different story; and then I retell it with his additions, and so we go on until no one could say whether it is more his story or mine.
— J. M. Barrie, *The Little White Bird*

Every afternoon James and Porthos waited in Kensington Gardens for the Davies boys and their nurse. While he waited, he jotted down observations and ideas in the pocket notebook he always carried with him:

> 225. *Annie's Boy.* Name printed on collar of green-grocer's cart-horse.
> 231. *Trees.* Chestnuts in park on windy day (May 20th)—petals of flowers falling like snow & covering ground—white with dot of red—sun shining on afterwards....
> 237. *Birds* (sparrows) in garden bathing in water pool made by hose—lying on back & kicking like dog.

Other notes revealed more about James himself:

> Woman who will always look glorious as a mother, (so I think of her *now*, always so). A woman to confide in

*Sylvia, mother of the
Llewelyn Davies boys*

(no sex in this, we feel it in man or woman). All secrets
of womanhood you feel behind these calm eyes & courage
to face them. A woman to lean on in trouble.

In *Tommy and Grizel* he expanded this note into a
beautiful description of Grizel that perfectly matched Sylvia
Llewelyn Davies.

It was the eldest Davies boy, George, who got most of
James's attention in the storytelling and games in Kensington
Gardens. He was a handsome and intelligent five-year-old, who
was innocent enough for make-believe yet old enough for
conversation. From their playing came notes for a book that
James called *The Little White Bird*. In it were recorded many
of the magical afternoons in the gardens.

When the 20th century arrived, James, now 40, could count 10 books and 7 plays among his successes. He was working on a new play, *Quality Street,* that his friend Charles

Quality Street *was first performed in the United States and starred Maude Adams. Hugh Thomson illustrated the book.*

Frohman planned to produce in America with Maude Adams as its star. It drew on James's childhood memories of the hanky school in Kirriemuir, but was written with a new mix of romantic comedy and gentle pathos that became Barrie's trademark in the theater.

In the summer of 1901, the Barries bought a car. They were the first in their group of friends to own a car, and they proudly showed it off. It was a steam "dog cart," with no top or windshield, powered by a boiler and steered by a tiller. James and Mary took turns driving it, but it often broke down. Some thought it was a miracle that it didn't also blow up! Later when James and Mary replaced it with a more reliable motor car, James lost interest in cars altogether. The dog cart had appealed to the child in him, but he detested more complex mechanical things. They hired a chauffeur. Then, more often than not, Mary went alone in the car while James walked or took the train.

People who knew them well began to notice that the Barries were gradually drifting apart. There were no children to tie them together, and Mary was often bored and restless while her husband locked himself away for hours and wrote. They could be charming and affectionate with each other when other people were around, but close observers suspected they were both just acting at those times.

The Barries had never planned to live in the city year-round, and now Mary began to look for a cottage in the country where they could spend their summers. She found a cottage on Black Lake near Farnham in Surrey, about 40 miles south of London. It needed a good deal of repair, so Mary supervised the renovations and James simply paid the bills. Mary transformed Black Lake Cottage into a peaceful retreat with flower gardens and broad green lawns stretching toward pine woods. It became a haven for James, who wrote in an upstairs room overlooking the lawns—and for the aging Porthos, who could roam without a leash.

Arthur and Sylvia Llewelyn Davies rented a summer house not far from Black Lake Cottage. There was now a new baby brother for George, Jack, and Peter. His name was Michael. The families saw each other every day that summer of 1901, and the games that had begun in Kensington Gardens went on to become more elaborate still.

Three Davies boys, ready for adventure, were photographed by James.

Here they had woods and a ruined abbey and a lake. A coral island emerged from James's imagination and anchored in the middle of Black Lake. The boys found themselves shipwrecked on it and in danger from pirates and wild animals. A tiger stalked them (he looked remarkably like Porthos wearing a paper mask). The climax came when the boys strung up the dastardly pirate, Captain Swarthy, a straw villain stuffed into a set of James's old clothes.

"George found himself within four feet of a tiger": Porthos wearing a paper mask.

Captain Swarthy is strung up, and the boys spend their last night on the island.

James was a skilled photographer, and he took pictures of these adventures and had them printed and bound into a book. He called it *The Boy Castaways of Black Lake Island: Being a Record of the Terrible Adventures of the Brothers Davies in the summer of 1901*. Only two copies were made, and one was quickly lost. In the surviving copy, James wrote an inscription: S Ll D & A Ll D from JMB. Underneath he wrote, "There was another copy of this book only and it was lost in a railway train in 1901."

James Barrie, as a middle-aged man, had discovered how to re-enter the world of boyhood, using real children as his guides.

"We trained the dog to watch over us while we slept."

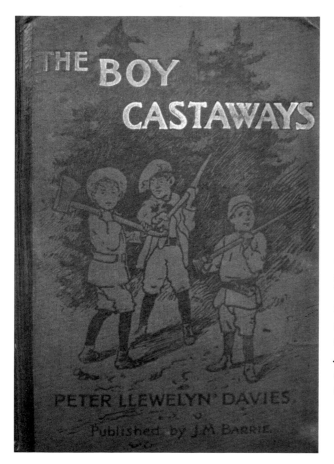

Of the two copies of The Boy Castaways, *only one survives. James credited Peter as the author.*

The boys' glorious summer came to an end. That autumn their great playfellow, Porthos, became ill. The Barries took him to a vet, but early the next morning they found the old dog standing outside their gate, his chain broken. Their hearts were broken, too, as they watched him grow weaker and finally die.

Arthur Rackham's illustrations for Peter Pan in Kensington Gardens *in 1906 set the style for "clothes worn by the people in fairydom." Here Rackham's fairies cavort over the Serpentine.*

TEN

Always the Same Age

1901–1903

*If you ask your mother whether she knew about Peter Pan
when she was a little girl, she will say, "Why, of course, I did,
child."...Peter is ever so old, but he is really always the same age.*
— J. M. Barrie, *The Little White Bird*

At Christmastime, James took the Davies boys to the
theater to see a sparkling new production called *Bluebell in
Fairyland*. It was described as a musical dream play, not the
traditional holiday pantomime for children. Soon afterward, jot-
tings appeared in James's notebook that showed he was beginning to plot a fantasy play for children. "Hero might be a poor
boy of today with ordinary clothes, unhappy, &c, in Act I.—
Taken to Fairydom still in everyday clothes which are strange
contrast to clothes worn by the people in fairydom—(a la Hans
Xian Andersen)." Another note was "Characters might be carried thro' the air on sheets borne by birds."

As 1902 began, he worked to finish another play for adults,
The Admirable Crichton, in which an upper-class English family is shipwrecked on an island with their butler, Crichton. They

owe their survival to Crichton, and he becomes the natural leader on the island. When they are rescued, however, they all revert—with discomfort—to their old class system.

American actor William Gillette created the role of the admirable Crichton in New York in 1903. The butler Crichton proves to be of sterner stuff than the aristocrats shipwrecked with him.

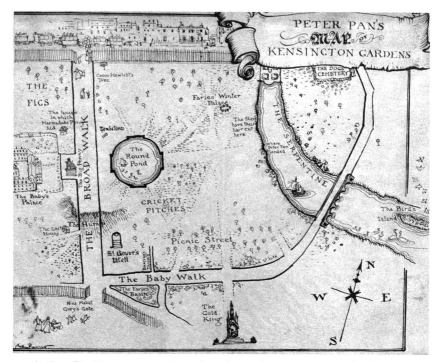

Arthur Rackham's map, based on James's story, created a fantasy world in Kensington Gardens.

At the same time, he continued to write chapters in *The Little White Bird*. He spun the fictional account of an old bachelor (himself) and David (who was really George Davies) around the adventures he and George still shared in Kensington Gardens. He added a mother (clearly based on Sylvia), a father (very like Arthur), and a multitude of other characters based on people they saw in the gardens.

But suddenly another boy appeared, right in the middle of the book.

His name was Peter Pan.

James wrote five chapters in *The Little White Bird* about Peter Pan, whom he introduced as a week-old baby. The

Peter Pan first appeared as a week-old baby in The Little White Bird. *In this Rackham painting, he rides out a storm in the thrush's nest.*

chapters explained how all the children in London had once been birds in Kensington Gardens and that people who wanted a child went there to try to "catch one with small pieces of cake." Peter Pan, it seemed, had flown out of his nursery window and gone back to the gardens when he was still in the bird stage, because he heard his parents talking about what he would become when he grew up. Peter had stayed away until dark. His grieving mother locked the nursery window and when Peter tried to get back in, he couldn't.

So the baby Peter went to live in Kensington Gardens, riding on a goat and playing the pan pipes, with the birds and fairies taking care of him. James called him "a Betwixt-and-Between"—not quite human, but not a bird, either.

The autumn of 1902 may have been the busiest season of James's career as an author and playwright. In September *Quality Street* opened in London after a successful run in the U.S. In November *The Admirable Crichton* opened in a neighboring theater. Then *The Little White Bird* was published.

That same autumn, James's father died in his 88th year. Mary and James went to Scotland to comfort his sister Sara and his uncle, both of whom had been living with James's father.

Mary convinced James that they should have a more stylish address, and they bought a larger house at No. 100 Bayswater Road, near Kensington Gardens. She threw herself into the renovation project. She created a private studio for James in the converted garage-stable behind the house.

After the hectic pace of the autumn months, James was ready for a change. To celebrate the successful run of his plays and the publication of *The Little White Bird,* the Barries took Sylvia Llewelyn Davies and another friend, the writer A. E. W. Mason, to Paris for a few glorious days. Arthur, left at home somewhat sourly to his father, "Sylvia is at present on a trip to Paris with her friends the Barries...and they seem to be living in great splendour and enjoying themselves very much." *Her* friends, Arthur said.

One day a very large green kennel appeared in the garden between the Barries' house and James's studio. Mary had bought a black-and-white Newfoundland puppy and she intended for it to stay in the kennel. The puppy would have none of it. "Shrieking is the only word to describe the noise that came from that kennel," Mary wrote. "I came to the conclusion that it was not possible to make a dog live in a kennel, if he didn't want to. That is, not in London, if you wish to keep the good-will of your neighbours." Soon the kennel disappeared.

They named the new dog Luath.

> Luath could be decidedly funny. He was funny with his master when he [James] came across the garden from his study at dinner-time. Every night when Luath heard him coming, he hid behind some bushes and as he passed along sprung out at him with a loud guffaw. It hardly ever failed to surprise his master, whose mind was still at work in his study.
>
> Then they both went 'mad dog' and scampered about the house, playing hide-and-seek in and out of rooms, and as most of the rooms led from one to another, a jolly fine time they had. For a quarter of an hour or so it was a perfect hullabaloo.

One day a letter arrived for James from the duke of Cambridge, who was also park ranger of Kensington Gardens. Enclosed in the letter was a key to the gardens for James's private use when the gates were closed to the public. This special honor was being awarded to him because of the fame brought to Kensington Gardens by *The Little White Bird*. James

The key to Kensington Gardens, for James's private use

was probably relieved to be able to walk in the gardens when there were no crowds around. Now that *The Little White Bird* was so popular, mothers were developing an annoying habit of watching for him and presenting their children to him in the hopes that he would write them into one of his stories.

On November 23, 1903, after months of careful note-taking and organizing, James wrote the first lines of *Anon—a Play*. It began in "the night nursery of the Darling family."

As the weeks passed, James's pen dipped swiftly in and out of the ink bottle, filling pages with the story of Peter Pan, whom he called "that sly one, the chief figure." James concentrated all his skills as a dramatist on capturing Peter and immortalizing him.

Peter and Wendy *was published in 1911, with illustrations by F. D. Bedford. This one is entitled "Hook or me—this time."*

ELEVEN

Writing the Play

1903–1904

I have no recollection of writing the play of Peter Pan.
— J. M. Barrie, dedication to *Peter Pan*

"Notwithstanding other possibilities, I think I wrote Peter, and if so it must have been in the usual inky way....I must have sat at a table with that great dog waiting for me to stop, not complaining, for he knew it was thus we made our living."

At one side of James's table was a pile of small sheets of paper containing carefully numbered notes. Referring to them as he wrote, he covered page after page of paper with his cramped handwriting. The first complete draft took him about four months to finish.

"The night nursery," began the stage directions. In his mind's eye, James saw the room at the Davieses' house where he so often watched the little boys play and protest as they were put to bed. It was only the night before James began to write when—by wonderful coincidence—a fifth boy, Nicholas, had been born to Sylvia and Arthur.

Sylvia Llewelyn Davies—the beautiful, idealized mother—was uppermost in his mind as he wrote about Mrs. Darling. "If only I had not accepted that invitation to dine," James has Mrs. Darling say. Was James remembering the dinner party when he first met the Davieses? How different their lives would have been if they had not accepted that invitation to dine.

And here came Nana, the dog nursery-maid, modeled on Porthos and Luath. Those huge, friendly dogs had romped with James and the boys over the years. Why not put them in the play, too? Luath loved children. And when Mr. Darling went to live in Nana's kennel, James was remembering the big green doghouse that Mary had bought for Luath.

A detachable shadow for Peter Pan—James remembered one in an old German tale about Peter Schlemihl. Flying children? Why not? All children dreamed at one time or another of being able to fly, and theaters already had reliable mechanical flying equipment. He soon engaged George Kirby of the Flying Ballet Company to design special harnesses for the actors.

Tinker Bell was born in James's imagination during the summer at Black Lake Island when he played at being pirates and castaways with the Davies boys. The baby, Michael, had waved his foot at a twinkling firefly one night, and the image remained with James.

He needed a name for the country where Peter took the Darling children. He had heard about a region in Australia with the unlikely name of Never Land, so that's where he sent them. But James's Never Land was like no other place on earth: it was populated with pirates, Indians, wolves, lost boys, and mermaids. The stories he had read over the years, the adventures he had played in Kirriemuir and Dumfries and Kensington Gardens—all went into the geography of his Never Land.

From his earliest childhood days came the stone wash

Michael Davies, "waving his foot at a firefly," was captured by James's camera.

house behind the Tenements, where he and his friend Robb produced their first plays. That would do fine for Wendy's little house. He would put John's hat on top of the wash boiler's chimney.

The name for his heroine must be unique, and he remembered a special name once given him by Margaret Henley, the daughter of William Ernest Henley. The child had died when she was only five. James wrote: "One might call it a sudden idea that came to her in the middle of her romping." She had tried to say James was her friend, but it came out "fwend" and then "fwendy" in her infant pronunciation. James made the change from fwendy to Wendy, and he had the name he wanted for his heroine.

James owned a painting of Margaret Henley, in which she was wearing a long cloak with a hood. In his play, Wendy would wear a cloak like this. Wendy's maternal personality, though, was more like that of his mother, Margaret Ogilvy. "I'm thinking I am in it again!" Margaret Ogilvy might very well have said to him.

Then of course there was Captain Hook, who first appeared in a slightly different form as Captain Swarthy in *The Boy Castaways of Black Lake Island*. Now he was Hook, first name James, and he smoked a cigar like J. M. Barrie did. The resemblance may not have stopped there. Captain Hook tries to capture Wendy and the Lost Boys. When the Davies boys grew up, one of them—Peter—said that James Barrie wanted to possess the people he most loved, and that included Sylvia and her family.

When he came to "that sly one, the chief figure," James created someone who never would have to "give up the games." Peter Pan was a cry from the heart of a man who longed for his lost boyhood. James portrayed Peter as carefree, innocent, and heartless—all those things he most admired in the children he knew. And in the end, he was "the tragic boy."

It is easy to trace the origins of most of the characters in *Peter Pan*. It is even possible to discover where Barrie's plots might have come from. But it is important, also, to see that Barrie himself was part of every character he created. The little Davies boys had helped him find "the golden ladder" that led back to boyhood. With his memories sharpened, and all his mature skills as a dramatist ready, he was able to create a play unlike any that had been written before.

Michael as Peter Pan and
James as Captain Hook

James had a Peter Pan costume made for Michael and then had him pose as a model for the Peter Pan statue in Kensington Gardens.

 TWELVE

Streaky with You Still

1904–1905

The play of Peter is streaky with you still, though none may see this save ourselves. A score of Acts had to be left out, and you were in them all.
— J. M. Barrie, dedication to *Peter Pan*

Now what was he to do with it?

Here was a play with expensive staging and a cast of nearly 50 actors. Its unusual mixture of reality and fairy tale, comedy and pathos, might not appeal to everybody—or to anybody. James first thought of the English producer Beerbohm Tree, who had done a lot of large-scale shows for the stage. He read it to Tree, who reacted quickly and negatively.

"Barrie has gone out of his mind," he tattled to James's American producer Charles Frohman.

> I am sorry to say it, but you ought to know it. He's just read me a play. He is going to read it to you, so I am warning you. I know I have not gone woozy in my mind, because I have tested myself since hearing the play; but Barrie must be mad.

James waited until April to show it to Frohman, when

85

the producer was in England for his annual visit. James had written a sure moneymaker called *Alice Sit-by-the-Fire*. He hoped that if he offered this to Frohman first, Frohman would be more likely to take on the riskier *Peter Pan*.

James needn't have worried. As soon as Frohman read *Peter Pan*, he was captivated. It went straight to the boy in him, and he never wavered in his excitement for the play. He immediately called for preparations to begin. No expense was to be spared.

John Crook composed a rollicking score and, according to the opening night program, W. Warde invented and arranged the dances. William Nicholson designed the sets and costumes, except for Peter Pan's, which were designed by Henry J. Ford. George Kirby's Flying Ballet Company made a new kind of harness to fly the actors.

Frohman hired Dion Boucicault to direct the production and then chose Dion's sister, Nina Boucicault, to play the part of Peter Pan. James had always hoped a male actor would play Peter, but Frohman convinced him to use the English pantomime tradition of having a woman play the principal boy, or hero. In addition, the roles of Michael and the Lost Boys were also given to women, mainly because child labor laws of the time said no actor younger than 14 years of age could be onstage after 9:00 P.M. A boy of 14 or older might play John Darling, but he would look too grown-up for Michael Darling and the younger Lost Boys, while a young woman of 14 could play the parts very well. Gerald du Maurier—Sylvia Llewelyn Davies's brother and uncle to the five Davies boys—was cast in the dual role of Captain Hook and Mr. Darling. Dorothea Baird played Mrs. Darling, and Hilda Trevelyan was the first Wendy. "There will never be another to touch you," Barrie wrote to her affectionately 16 years later.

The original cast of Peter Pan

Michael Darling riding Nana

Arthur Lupino played the part of Nana and went to the Barries' house to be instructed by Luath, the Newfoundland. "He showed [Lupino] how to walk," Mary wrote, "to express emotion by the wag of his tail and also by barking. Then there was the beating on the floor with his feet—dancing I called it— when especially pleased." It was Luath's black-and-white coat that was copied by a costume designer at a cost of 30 guineas, an extravagant amount of money in 1904.

Nina Boucicault as Peter Pan, dressed as Napoleon after defeating Captain Hook

One night the real dog took a curtain call at the theater. When the audience realized they were looking at Luath and not the actor, a shout went up, followed by an answering roar from Luath. After that, Mary related, "he was quite famous in the Kensington Gardens, and the liberties he took unchallenged by the nurses were beyond belief. I have seen him take a bun out of the hand of a baby in a perambulator and eat it."

Peter Pan has been in production somewhere in the world almost continuously since 1904. It has been translated into French, German, and Italian, among other languages. Actors stayed with the English production for record lengths of time. George Shelton, the original Smee, played the part for 24 years; and William Luff, who started as Cecco and then was Captain Hook, was in the production for 45 years.

One actor's name—Jane (sometimes Jenny) Wren—has remained on every playbill since 1904 in the role of Tinker Bell. Jane Wren is a spotlight reflected from a mirror, and her voice is a collar of bells. The original two bells for her famous line, "You silly ass," were brought by James from Switzerland.

Of course, not everyone loved *Peter Pan*. Some agreed with Beerbohm Tree's first opinion that the author was mad. One cartoon caricatured James reading the play to a group of children and adults. The children were all asleep. George Bernard Shaw called it an artificial freak foisted on children by the grown-ups.

When Maude Adams created the part of Peter Pan in the United States in 1905, one reviewer wrote: "This Peter Pan is described as a fantasy. It is more; it is a nightmare."

Americans generally loved the play, however. Mark Twain wrote a letter to Maude Adams saying, "It is my belief that *Peter Pan* is a great and refining and uplifting benefaction to this sordid and money-mad age; and that the next best play

Maude Adams as Peter Pan

on the boards is a long way behind it as long as you play Peter."

James did not wish to have the play published right away, and it was 25 years before there was anything but a production script to read. One reason, perhaps, is that the author continually revised the lines every time a new production was in rehearsal. When he finally agreed to have it published in 1928, he added a moving dedication "To the Five" Davies boys, without whom Peter Pan never would have existed. "I hope, my dear sirs, that in memory of what we have been to each other you will accept this dedication with your friend's love."

Cecilia Loftus played Peter Pan in the second London production in 1905. This illustration shows the costumes designed for it.

The Barrie and Llewelyn Davies families spent summers near each other in Surrey. Here James entertains five-year-old Michael on the lawn at Black Lake Cottage in 1905.

THIRTEEN

Their Boys (My Boys)

1905–1910

To Sylvia and Arthur Llewelyn Davies
and Their Boys (My Boys)
—J. M. Barrie, *Peter Pan in Kensington Gardens*

James knew the public also wanted to read about Peter Pan. So two years after the play opened, he took the chapters from *The Little White Bird* where Peter Pan first appeared as a baby and had them published as *Peter Pan in Kensington Gardens*. The book was illustrated with stunning, full-color paintings—50 of them—drawn by Arthur Rackham, whom James commissioned for the job. It was the bestselling Christmas gift book of 1906 and set a new standard for illustrated children's books. Rackham worked on the pictures for nearly a year and sketched many of them in Kensington Gardens themselves. When they were finished, he wrote to James and asked for a meeting so he could show the paintings to him.

James's reply, in June 1906, apologized for a delay in answering, explaining, "I am so much at present with a friend who is dangerously ill that I have not seen my letters till now."

One of Rackham's fairies in Peter Pan in Kensington Gardens, *"looking very undancey indeed" and also looking very much like Sylvia*

The friend was Arthur Llewelyn Davies, who was dying from cancer. James spent nearly all his days at the hospital to help with Arthur's care. He paid the medical fees and other expenses. Arthur had not yet accumulated much wealth from his law practice and had nothing to fall back upon in an emergency. Except James Barrie. Arthur must have been uncomfortable with being dependent on James, but as he grew weaker, he also became very grateful to the compassionate and possessive man who insisted on taking over responsibility for Sylvia and the boys.

Peter Pan in Kensington Gardens was released at the end of 1906. On the dedication page were these words: "To Sylvia and Arthur Llewelyn Davies and Their Boys (My Boys)." Four months later Arthur was dead.

James bought a house for Sylvia and the boys close to his own in London. The Davieses had been living 25 miles away in the country for several years. Mary Barrie did not seem to resent her husband's involvement with the Davies family. She was still fond of Sylvia, and she knew James would do what he wanted to anyway.

For some time, rumors about trouble in the Barries' marriage had been circulating. They had their separate friends and activities, and Mary had even set up a studio away from home where she worked producing artistic enamel-ware. Her husband was very rich and very generous to her and others. But no amount of wealth could buy back the first happy years of their marriage.

Suddenly she announced that she wanted a divorce. She was in love with Gilbert Cannan, a young aspiring dramatist, and wished to marry him. Divorce laws in England at that time required that James prove she had been unfaithful to him. It was a terrible blow to his pride. A group of his influential friends—including Henry James, A. E. W. Mason, H. G. Wells, and Beerbohm Tree—asked the newspapers to keep the matter quiet; otherwise it would have caused a great scandal.

"She could tell no more than I why she had ceased to love me," James had written a few years earlier in *The Little White Bird*. "The failure was mine alone." Sadly, what James wrote as fiction seemed to have come true for him.

In the divorce settlement, James gave Mary the cottage at Black Lake, the cars they owned, and even Luath. He was stunned. Devoted friends moved him from the house near Kensington Gardens into an apartment near the theater district, in Adelphi Terrace House. And they helped him hire a couple to be butler and cook.

Two days after the Barries' divorce settlement, Sylvia Llewelyn Davies collapsed on the stairs of her house. A doctor diagnosed an advanced, inoperable cancer. The doctor did

After James and Mary divorced in 1909, he moved into Adelphi Terrace House.

Sylvia du
Maurier
Llewelyn Davies

not want her or her boys to know how seriously ill she was, but James was told, as were members of her household staff.

A time of watching and waiting began, as the enchanting Sylvia slipped away from her five sons and the adoring James. In her will, written shortly before her death a year later in August 1910, she wrote: "J. M. B. I know will do everything in his power to help our boys—to advise, to comfort, to sympathise in all their joys & sorrows."

James Barrie with the duchess of Sutherland and four of the Llewelyn Davies boys in 1911. Back row (left to right): George, *age 18; the duchess; and* Peter, *age 14. Front row:* Nico, *age 7;* James, *age 51; and* Michael, *age 11.*

FOURTEEN

Roses in December

1910–1918

*You remember someone said that God gave us memory
so that we might have roses in December.*
—J. M. Barrie, *Courage*

At the age of 50, James Barrie became the guardian and sole support of five boys, ages 7 to 17. George, the eldest, was away studying at Eton and preparing for Cambridge. Jack was in the naval college at Dartmouth, and Peter was just starting at Eton. The two youngest were at home: Michael was 10 and Nicholas—called Nico—was 7.

Home for the boys was still the house near Kensington Gardens that James had bought for them and Sylvia when Arthur died. Now Mary Hodgson, the loyal nursemaid who had been with the boys since George's infancy, took care of it; and James was a frequent visitor. Mary Hodgson still did not really like James, but she had to tolerate him because now he was clearly in charge.

James was working on a storybook called *Peter and Wendy*, based on *Peter Pan*. In it are many poignant references to

99

mothers dying and children being brought up by someone with no experience. Having boys of his own might have been what James always wanted, but when the time came, it was much different from what he expected. The boys never lacked for anything that money could buy. A lot of people said James spoiled them. But who could blame him for wanting to give everything to the children of Arthur and Sylvia?

The next year, a much-publicized tragedy put yet another young boy into his protection. James was godfather to Peter Scott, son of the explorer Robert Falcon Scott. When Scott died at the South Pole, a letter addressed to James was found on his frozen body. It asked James to "be good to my wife and child. Give the boy a chance in life...." And of course, James did all he could for Peter and his mother for many years.

As the fame of *Peter Pan* continued to spread, James arranged a surprise for the children who played in Kensington Gardens. When the gates opened on the morning of May 1,

The widow and son of explorer Robert Falcon Scott

Fantasy creatures swarm toward the bronze Peter Pan in Kensington Gardens.

1912, visitors saw that a large bronze statue of Peter Pan had appeared as if by magic near the Round Pond. James had commissioned the sculptor Sir George Frampton to make the statue and had paid for it himself. The statue was supposed to have been modeled after Michael Llewelyn Davies, dressed in a Peter Pan costume. But Frampton chose another boy instead, and James was never quite satisfied. "It doesn't show the Devil in Peter," he complained.

One night James, at home with 10-year-old Nico, told Nico "to look in the papers the next morning for surprising news, and he was up betimes and searched the cricket columns from end to end." But he missed the news: James Matthew Barrie had been named a literary baronet in the Birthday Honours list. Henceforth, he was Sir J. M. Barrie, Bart. Bart was short for baronet. The Davies boys began to refer to him as the Bart when they weren't saying Uncle Jim.

Britain moved closer and closer to war with Germany, and in August 1914 it came. Shortly afterward, British writers— J. M. Barrie, Thomas Hardy, H. G. Wells, and many others— were summoned to a meeting with a government official. They were asked to do all they could through their writing to build support for the growing British involvement in the war. James responded by writing several short stories and plays during the next few years that raised funds and enthusiasm for the war effort. Among these were *The Old Lady Shows Her Medals, A Well-Remembered Voice, Der Tag,* and *Barbara's Wedding.*

In addition, James decided he could be of further help by going to the United States and trying to change its neutrality about the war into support for Britain and its allies. A British government official authorized this secret and somewhat romanticized mission. James and two friends, T. L. Gilmour and A. E. W. Mason, sailed for New York on the *Lusitania* in September. The ship was so full of Americans leaving Europe to get away from the war that the only room available for James and his friends was the children's playroom, re-fitted with berths. Somehow, the newspapers found out about James's mission, and when he arrived in New York, he was given a message from the British ambassador telling him to abandon the mission because it might embarrass the British government.

When reporters came to interview James, he told them that he had come on a private visit. He did, in fact, spend a most enjoyable four weeks. He visited his old friend Charles

Frohman and saw Maude Adams act in one of his plays. He saw many films and plays and dined with American authors and journalists at their clubs. Former U.S. president Theodore Roosevelt invited James to his home at Oyster Bay, Long Island.

"Roosevelt was an entrancing personality, but such a talker that I could not get in a word. The last I saw of him he was running and talking alongside the little carriage that took me to the station. Gradually we out-distanced his voice."

Suddenly—and shockingly—the war entered James's life and ended his delusions about it. Guy du Maurier, brother to Sylvia Llewelyn Davies and Gerald du Maurier, was killed in battle.

Within a week came the most terrible news of all: George Llewelyn Davies was killed in action in France. James would call the eldest of the five brothers "the most gallant of you all." And now he was dead. James received George's last letter—written from the battlefield just hours before he was shot—on the following day, along with a telegram of condolence from King George and Queen Mary.

Two months later, a German torpedo sank the *Lusitania* on its way to Europe—and James's great friend Charles Frohman went to his death, another victim of the war.

The casualty list went on and on. James's two nephews, the sons of his brother Alexander, died, as did the sons and brothers of many of his friends. Peter Llewelyn Davies was shell-shocked and sent home for a long, slow period of recovery.

From his apartment on Adelphi Terrace overlooking the Thames River, James could see giant searchlights sweeping the night sky for signs of Zeppelins or Gothas. Air raids came so close that he sometimes found shrapnel on his balcony.

James gave tremendous amounts of energy and money to the war effort. Friends opened a hospital for convalescent soldiers at their country estate, and James sent thousands of pounds for its support, then went himself to entertain the patients and staff.

He was haunted by stories of wounded and orphaned children in France, so he arranged for other friends to go at his expense to an abandoned chateau near Bettancourt and establish a refuge for them. He supplied money for all its needs and went there to support and encourage whenever he could.

Another person whom he had once loved—Mary Ansell —came back into his life toward the end of the war. Mary's marriage to Gilbert Cannan had ended, and she had returned to London to work in a hospital depot making bandages. She had been forced to sell Black Lake Cottage for her living expenses, and she was in desperate need. James arranged for an allowance to be paid to her for life. After the war, Mary moved to France, and on her occasional visits to London in later years, James and Mary saw each other.

As the war drew to an end, James would pace back and forth in his rooms overlooking the Thames. He smoked his pipe, and he coughed, and he went over his notes trying to find an idea for a play that would engage his interest.

Then his friend A. E. W. Mason reminded him of a plot they had discussed years earlier. What about a group of people who are given a second chance in life to choose what they would do? The idea struck an immediate response in James. To have a second chance. What he and the world wouldn't give for a second chance in this final, terrible year of the war! He started to work almost at once, organizing the pile of notes for *Dear Brutus,* which became one of his most enduring plays.

Magic took over his pen once more. This time the main character was Lob, a sinister little old man with mystical powers who seems like an ancient Peter Pan. Lob invites a group of

William Gillette starred as the childless man and Helen Hayes as his dream daughter in Dear Brutus.

people to his country house on Midsummer's Eve and tricks them into entering a mysterious wood that suddenly appears outside his house.

Under the wood's spell, the people forget who they are and make new choices of love and work. Unfortunately, they make the same kinds of mistakes all over again. Only one, a childless man who finds a daughter—a dream child—is truly happy in the enchanted wood. James, still the master of stagecraft, was writing with a sadder and wiser pen.

James, being short, could walk into his inglenook—the nook by the fireplace—without bumping his head, but visitors couldn't. He often curled up to read on the uncomfortable leather sofa—like Lob in Dear Brutus.

FIFTEEN

The One Left
1918–1921

Yes indeed it is the one left who is struck dead.
— J. M. Barrie to Mrs. Lewis

"If you really want a job, why not come and help me?"

"Help you," I mumbled. "Er...Er...How?"

"My papers are getting into an awful mess," he said. "I must have someone to cope with them, but I don't want what agents call 'professional efficiency.'"

"But I can't type!"

"I could never stand the clatter of a typewriter," said Barrie.

This is how Lady Cynthia Asquith described her invitation, in the summer of 1918, to become James's secretary. James needed help with the appalling muddle of his papers, and Cynthia, the beautiful younger daughter of an earl and daughter-in-law of a former prime minister, needed the money while her husband was away at the war front.

Cynthia remained James's devoted secretary and friend for the rest of his life. She later described her employer as he was when they first met:

He's curiously like a charcoal drawing. I'm surprised by
the extreme blueness of his eyes in daylight. I notice
for the first time how finely modelled his nose is, how
much strength as well as sensitiveness there is in his
face.... His words are frequently interrupted by smoker's
spluttering, sometimes by collision with a cough. His
voice, with that queer rumbling burr in it, is always
deep, often rather hoarse; in his longer sentences a little
sing-song.

*James basks in
the devoted
gaze of his new
secretary, Lady
Cynthia Asquith.*

James was photographed at a coffee stall on the Embankment one night in 1921. He had been awakened by the bright lights of a film crew making a movie and went out to watch.

James once commented about his cough (although one had better not comment to him about it): "I suppose it's like Big Ben, not quite as loud, but so frequent that I've ceased to notice it."

James was starting to work on a new play, to be called *Mary Rose,* when writer's cramp forced him to stop using his right hand and train his left to take over. Cynthia wrote: "I remember his announcing this change quite formally, as though in dismissing his right hand he were giving notice to a servant of many years faithful service."

Mary Rose is a haunting tale about a young mother who is spirited away by a call from an enchanted island and returns as a ghost years later to look for her baby. She is still young—like a wistful Peter Pan—but the baby is a grown man whom she thinks is an intruder.

His left hand, James said, "seems to have a darker and more sinister outlook on life, and is trying at present to egg me on to making a woman knife her son." In many ways, James's whole life was growing darker.

One evening in May 1921, James went down from his apartment to mail his daily letter to Michael Davies, then studying at Oxford. A reporter met him at the door and asked if he could add any details about what had happened. James had no idea what the man was referring to. So the reporter told him the awful news: Michael and a classmate had drowned that afternoon in a pond at Oxford.

"The Mortal Blow had fallen," a friend wrote. "He never got over it. It altered and darkened everything for the rest of his life."

It was Cynthia who saved James's sanity, and possibly his life, during the days that followed. He "looked like a man in a nightmare," she wrote in her diary.

Michael had been James's shining hope. The brilliant, personable 21-year-old had inherited the best qualities of both his parents. He had been James's favorite among the five brothers.

"For ever and ever I am thinking about him," James sadly wrote to friends. "Michael was pretty much my world....what

THE POOL OF ILL-OMEN : TRAGEDY REPEATED AFTER 78 YEARS.

Sandford Pool, Oxford, where Mr. Michael Llewellyn Davies (inset) and Mr. Rupert Buxton, both undergraduates, were drowned while bathing. The bodies were recovered yesterday. Mr. Davies was one of Sir James Barrie's adopted sons; the other, believed to be the original of "Peter Pan," was killed in action. The monument in the picture commemorates two other Oxford men drowned there in 1843.

When Michael drowned while a student at Oxford University, newspapers identified him as Sir James Barrie's adopted son. James never fully recovered from his grief at Michael's death.

happened was in a way the end of me." He may have been thinking of Michael when he wrote in his 1928 dedication to *Peter Pan:* "There is Peter still, but to me he lies sunk in the gay Black Lake."

Streamers and confetti—as well as titles, degrees, and other honors—were showered on Sir J. M. Barrie during his later years in recognition of his great literary achievements.

SIXTEEN

A Weaver All My Life

1921–1937

When I left my beloved little native town—a weaving
town then—I little thought that I was going to be a weaver
all my life. All the others have now given weaving up,
and I am the only weaver left.
— J. M. Barrie, *M'Connachie and J. M. B.*

James gradually recovered from his grief over Michael's death. Although he had always been quick to go to the relief of anyone in trouble, the tragedy in his own life now made him even more sensitive to the suffering of others. Only he would ever know how much money he gave to support the widows and children of his fellow authors or how many poor young artists benefited from his anonymous support.

In 1922 James's three-year term as rector of St. Andrew's University in Scotland was ending, and he was scheduled to give his rectorial address. He felt a great responsibility to say something significant to the students. During the weeks he spent working on the speech he called "Courage," he was filled with nervous apprehension. Michael's death was still painfully fresh, and these young undergraduates were just Michael's age.

The ceremony started badly. When James got up to speak, he somehow picked up a large letter opener from the table in front of him and fiddled with it as he started to speak. His voice was low and nervous. The young men in the audience could hardly hear him and were growing restless. James began to look desperate.

Suddenly, from the back of the room, one of the students shouted out, "Put it down, Jamie, or you'll cut your throat!" This glorious insolence of the young, which always delighted James, galvanized him into action. He began again, and this time he spoke with such power that his audience was deeply moved. James pulled Robert Falcon Scott's letter from his pocket and read to them the ringing words of courage from the dying hero: "We are in a desperate state—feet frozen, etc., no fuel, and a long way from food, but it would do your heart good to be in our tent, to hear our songs and our cheery conversation."

James reminded the students of the classmates they had lost in the recent world war: "The war has done at least one big thing: it has taken spring out of the year....The spring of the year lies buried in the fields of France and elsewhere."

"Brave words, wrapped in magic," was the judgment of more than one who heard them. Wave after wave of applause engulfed James. It was a triumphal day for him.

As one of Britain's leading literary figures, James was becoming a public figure, even though he detested public scrutiny of his private life. In the next years, he was asked to preside at many charitable events and to speak at dinners honoring notable people. He was invited to write prefaces to books and give eulogies in memory of the famous. James developed a fascinating new form of expression: writing stage directions for editions of his collected plays. He earned praise for generous donations of his original manuscripts to be auctioned for worthy causes.

In 1922 James proudly accepted the Order of Merit, awarded annually by the king. When he went to the investiture to receive his red-and-blue enameled badge, he jokingly

James was a great fan of cricket and was noted for his slow left bowl, here delivered at Dundee University in 1922.

complained about having to wear knee breeches. "Yes, I had to go to Buckingham Palace and in *knee-breeches* (closed car and sneaked to and fro like a burglar). My stockings misbehaved and creased like a concertina."

In 1929 James was asked to serve on a committee of the Great Ormond Street Hospital for Sick Children in London. He declined, but said he would think of another way of helping the hospital. In April 1929, James gave the hospital all the rights and royalties to *Peter Pan*—both the play and the books. This Peter Pan Gift, as it is called, continues as long as the hospital exists. It was James's stipulation that the sum earned from *Peter Pan* would never be revealed, but it is clearly of substantial benefit to the hospital.

He followed Thomas Hardy as president of the Incorporated Society of Authors and Composers. He was made honorary chancellor of Edinburgh University. He dined with the prime minister at No. 10 Downing Street, and he even had tea with the royal princesses.

Kirriemuir is just a few miles from Glamis Castle, where the duke and duchess of York—who in 1936 would become King George VI and Queen Elizabeth—spent their holidays. James was in Scotland in August of 1933 when Princess Margaret Rose celebrated her third birthday. The royal family invited Sir J. M. Barrie to the party.

He had the seat of honor next to the princess as she looked at her gifts, and later he wrote about it:

> She was in a frenzy of glee about them, especially about one to which she had given the place of honour by her plate. I said to her as one astounded "Is that really your very own?" and she saw how I envied her and immediately placed it between us with the words "It is yours—and mine."

Princesses Elizabeth and Margaret Rose with their mother in 1937

Later, when someone mentioned James Barrie's name, she said, "I know that man. He is my greatest friend, and I am *his* greatest friend." At the age of 73, James could still put children under his spell.

James had seen the German actress Elisabeth Bergner onstage, and he wanted to write a play for her. She told him she had always wanted to play the part of the boy King David, so James began to work on it. Out came the notebooks and the piles of paper with numbered notes. He worked long hours for many weeks. But he was 76 years old, and the emotional shocks of the last years had taken their toll on his body, still wracked by coughs.

James finished the play, *The Boy David,* and it went into production. He was absent from some of the critical rehearsals because he was ill, and when the play finally opened its trial run in Edinburgh at the end of 1936, it lacked the Barrie magic. It closed after only six weeks.

In the spring of 1937, James's life was marked by increasing pain. Neuritis, the doctors said, or lumbago. But they weren't certain. There were periods when he was too ill to leave his bed. James continued to correspond with friends and even enjoyed occasional days when he felt quite well and was again a charming and high-spirited companion.

He loved to have Cynthia read aloud to him. He never tired

James holds Nico Llewelyn Davies's daughter Laura.

of listening to books by Jane Austen, Emily Brontë, and Charles Dickens. He thought the Crummlies, a fictional family of actors in Dickens's *Nicholas Nickleby,* were the best comic characters in all literature. And he asked Cynthia to read over and over again A. E. Housman's *A Shropshire Lad,* with its moving verses about young heroes.

Word had reached King George that his friend Sir James was very ill. He remembered when James had told Princess Margaret Rose that the words she spoke to him at her third birthday party were going to be in his play *The Boy David.* And James had promised the princess a penny for every time the lines were used onstage. Now the king wrote to James with a playfulness that gave James's spirits a lift. If he didn't pay up, he would be hearing from the king's solicitors! With Cynthia's help, James set about arranging for a formal document of collaboration to be drawn up by his solicitor. He sent to the bank for a bag of new pennies, which he and Cynthia intended to deliver to the palace in person.

In May, James celebrated his 77th birthday by taking Cynthia to the Savoy for dinner, as he had done for years. He made plans to take Cynthia and her husband with him to Italy in mid-June for a holiday with Elisabeth Bergner.

Three days before his appointment to deliver the pennies to the princess, James became so ill that his doctors decided to move him to a nursing home. He lingered for 10 more days, in and out of consciousness. He did not know that Mary Ansell came all the way from her home in Biarritz, France, to see him one last time. Then on June 19, 1937, he died in his sleep.

For the last time, Jamie Barrie went up the winding road to the cemetery on the hill above his little red town of Kirriemuir. His neighbors accompanied him. Long ago they had forgiven him for the Scotch things in his early books that had offended them. Now they were proud to claim him as a favorite son. His childhood friend Mills was one of the pallbearers. James was laid to rest in the grave with his family. On the tombstone, beneath their names, is the simple inscription: James Matthew Barrie—9th May, 1860 – 19 June, 1937.

At the same hour as the funeral in Kirriemuir, more than 600 people attended a memorial service in Edinburgh for Sir James Barrie, Baronet, Order of Merit, chancellor of the University. A week after that, another great crowd gathered in London at St. Paul's Cathedral to hear the archbishop of Canterbury pay tribute to the brilliant little man from Scotland. J. M. Barrie had bought "a penny bottle of ink to heave at the metropolis" half a century before and had stayed on to become one of its most honored men of letters.

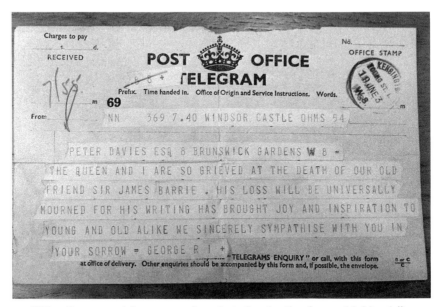

"The Queen and I are so grieved at the death of our old friend,"
wrote King George VI to Peter Llewelyn Davies on June 19,
1937.

Children still believe in the magic of Peter Pan, nearly a century after James Barrie's pen first captured him on paper. And Peter Pan—never to grow old—still plays his pipes in Kensington Gardens.

Sources

p.7   J. M. Barrie, *Peter Pan: Or the Boy Who Would Not Grow Up* (New York: Charles Scribner's Sons, 1928), vii. Reprinted with permission of Charles Scribner's Sons, an imprint of Macmillan Publishing Company. Copyright 1928 J. M. Barrie; copyright renewed 1956 Lady Cynthia Asquith, Peter Llewelyn Davies, and Barclay Bank Ltd.

p.7   Ibid., 121.

p.7   Ibid., 122.

p.8   Viola Meynell, ed., *Letters of James M. Barrie* (New York: Charles Scribner's Sons, 1947), 18.

p.8   Cynthia Asquith, *Portrait of Barrie* (London: James Barrie, 1954), 19. Reprinted with permission of E. P. Dutton, an imprint of Penguin U.S.A.

p.10   Barrie, *Peter Pan*, vi.

p.10   Ibid., 7.

p.11   Telegram to Charles Frohman.

p.13   J. M. Barrie, preface to *The Coral Island* (London: James Nisbet, 1913).

p.13   J. M. Barrie, *Margaret Ogilvy* (New York: Charles Scribner's Sons, 1946), 1. Reprinted with permission of Charles Scribner's Sons, an imprint of Macmillan Publishing Company (New York, 1896).

p.13   J. M. Cockburn, *A Birthplace in Thrums* (Edinburgh: National Trust for Scotland, 1964).

p.13   Barrie, *Margaret Ogilvy*, 1.

p.13   Ibid., 1, 3.

p.17   Ibid., 6.

p.17   Ibid.

p.17   Barrie, *Margaret Ogilvy*, 6.

p.17   Ibid., 12.

p.17   Ibid.

p.17   Ibid., 13.

p.19   Ibid., 42.

pp.21–22   Ibid., 45.

p.22   Ibid., 47.

p.22   Ibid.

p.22   Ibid., 48.

p.23   Ibid., 48-49.

p.23   Ibid., 49.

p.23   Ibid., 50-51.

p.23   Ibid., 30.

p.25   J. M. Barrie, *The Greenwood Hat* (New York: Charles Scribner's Sons, 1938), 25. Reprinted with permission of Charles Scribner's Sons, an imprint of Macmillan Publishing Company. Copyright 1938 Cynthia Asquith.

p.25   J. M. Barrie, *M'Connachie and J. M. B.* (New York: Charles Scribner's Sons, 1939), 77. Reprinted with permission of Charles Scribner's Sons, an imprint of Macmillan Publishing Company. Copyright 1938, 1939 Charles Scribner's Sons.

p.25   Barrie, preface to *The Coral Island*.

p.25   Denis Mackail, *The Story of J. M. B.* (London: Peter Davies, 1941), 41. Reprinted with permission of his daughter, Mary Mackail Oliphant.

pp.25–26   Ibid.

p.26   Barrie, *M'Connachie and J. M. B.*, 80-81.

p.26   J. A. Hammerton, *Barrie: The Story of a Genius* (New York: Dodd, Mead, 1929), 60.

p.27   Mackail, *The Story of J. M. B.*, 41.

p.27   Ibid., 42.

p.28 Barrie, *Margaret Ogilvy,* 93.
p.28 Ibid., 94.
p.28 Ibid.
p.28 Ibid., 93.
p.30 Ibid., 62.
p.31 Ibid., 63-64.
p.31 Ibid., 64.
p.31 Ibid., 65.
p.32 Barrie, *The Greenwood Hat,* 7.
p.33 Barrie, *Margaret Ogilvy,* 71.
p.33 Ibid.
p.33 Ibid., 56-57.
p.33 Barrie, *The Greenwood Hat,* 16.
p.35 Barrie, *M'Connachie and J. M. B.,* 230.
pp.35–36 Barrie, *Margaret Ogilvy,* 58-59.
p.36 Barrie, *The Greenwood Hat,* 18.
p.36 Ibid.
p.36 Ibid., 20.
p.36 Ibid., 26.
p.36 Ibid., 272.
p.36 Ibid.
p.37 Barrie, *M'Connachie and J. M. B.,* 161.
p.37 Barrie, *The Greenwood Hat,* 154.
p.39 Barrie, *M'Connachie and J. M. B.,* 230.
p.39 Ibid.
p.41 J. M. Barrie, *Tommy and Grizel* (London: Cassell, 1896), 117.
p.41 Barrie, *Margaret Ogilvy,* 30.
p.41 Ibid., 146.
p.42 J. M. Barrie, *The Little White Bird* (New York: Charles Scribner's Sons, 1913), 103. Reprinted with permission of Charles Scribner's Sons, an imprint of Macmillan Publishing Company. Copyright 1902 Charles Scribner's Sons; copyright renewed 1930 J. M. Barrie.
p.42 Ibid.
p.43 Barrie, *M'Connachie and J. M. B.,* 57.

p.44 Barrie, *The Greenwood Hat,* 267.
p.44 Ibid., 207.
p.47 Mary Ansell, *Of Dogs and Men* (London: Duckworth, 1923), 4.
p.47 Ibid., 10.
p.47 Ibid., 18.
p.49 Barrie, *Margaret Ogilvy,* 203.
p.49 Ibid., 185.
p.50 Ibid., 203.
p.50 Ibid., 204.
p.50 *British Weekly,* December 1896.
p.50 George Blake, *Barrie and the Kailyard School* (New York: Roy Publishers, 1951), 73.
p.53 Barrie, *The Little White Bird,* 120-21.
p.53 *New York Times,* 2 October 1896. Reprinted courtesy of The New York Times Company.
p.53 Ibid., 4 October 1896.
pp.53–54 Ibid.
p.61 Barrie, *The Little White Bird,* 132-3.
p.61 Mackail, *The Story of J. M. B.,* 243-4.
pp.61–62 Andrew Birkin, *J. M. Barrie & the Lost Boys: The Love Story that Gave Birth to Peter Pan* (New York: Clarkson N. Potter, 1979), 60.
p.68 J. M. Barrie, "The Boy Castaways," J. M. Barrie Collection, Beinecke Rare Book and Manuscript Library, Yale University.
p.71 Barrie, *The Little White Bird,* 131.
p.71 Birkin, *J. M. Barrie & the Lost Boys,* 93.
p.71 Ibid.
p.75 Barrie, *The Little White Bird,* 22.
p.75 Ibid., 138.
p.76 Birkin, *J. M. Barrie & the Lost Boys,* 96.

p.76   Ansell, *Of Dogs and Men,* 47.

p.76   Ibid., 68.

p.77   Barrie, *Peter Pan,* 3.

p.77   Ibid., xxvii.

p.79   Ibid., viii.

p.79   Ibid., xii.

p.79   Ibid., 3.

p.80   J. M. Barrie, *Peter Pan and Wendy* (New York: Charles Scribner's Sons, 1928), 14.

p.81   Barrie, *The Greenwood Hat,* 185.

p.82   Barrie, *Margaret Ogilvy,* 185.

p.82   Barrie, *Peter Pan,* xxvii.

p.82   Barrie, *Margaret Ogilvy,* 29.

p.82   Barrie, *The Little White Bird,* 203.

p.82   Barrie, *Tommy and Grizel,* 76.

p.85   Barrie, *Peter Pan,* v.

p.85   Phyllis Robbins, *Maude Adams: An Intimate Portrait* (New York: Putnam, 1956), 90.

p.85   Ibid.

p.86   Roger Lancelyn Green, *Fifty Years of Peter Pan* (London: Peter Davies, 1954), 92.

p.88   Ansell, *Of Dogs and Men,* 64.

p.89   Ibid.

p.89   Barrie, *Peter Pan.*

p.89   *Washington Star,* 22 October 1905.

pp.89–90   Robbins, *Maude Adams,* 90, 92.

pp.90–91   Barrie, *Peter Pan,* v.

p.93   J. M. Barrie, *Peter Pan in Kensington Gardens* (New York: Charles Scribner's Sons, 1906).

p.93   Derek Hudson, *Arthur Rackham: His Life and Work* (New York: Charles Scribner's Sons, 1960), 62.

p.95   Barrie, *Peter Pan in Kensington Gardens.*

'p.96   Barrie, *The Little White Bird,* 90.

p.97   Birkin, *J. M. Barrie & the Lost Boys,* 189.

p.99   J. M. Barrie, *Courage* (New York: Charles Scribner's Sons, 1922), 1.

p.100   Mackail, *The Story of J. M. B.,* 451.

p.101   Birkin, *J. M. Barrie & the Lost Boys,* 202.

pp.101–102   Meynell, *Letters of James M. Barrie,* 69.

p.103   Barrie, *The Greenwood Hat,* 193.

p.103   Barrie, *Peter Pan,* vii.

p.107   Meynell, *Letters of James M. Barrie,* 128.

p.107   Asquith, *Portrait of Barrie,* 4.

p.108   Ibid., 9-10.

p.109   Meynell, *Letters of James M. Barrie,* 159.

p.109   Asquith, *Portrait of Barrie,* 45.

p.110   Meynell, *Letters of James M. Barrie,* 130.

p.110   Mackail, *The Story of J. M. B.,* 560.

p.110   Birkin, *J. M. Barrie & the Lost Boys,* 293.

p.110   Meynell, *Letters of James M. Barrie,* 193.

pp.110–111   Birkin, *J. M. Barrie & the Lost Boys,* 295.

p.111   Barrie, *Peter Pan,* x.

p.113   Barrie, *M'Connachie and J. M. B.,* 222.

p.114   Mackail, *The Story of J. M. B.,* 573.

p.114   Barrie, *Courage,* 32.

p.114   Ibid., 15.

p.114   Mackail, *The Story of J. M. B.,* 574.

p.116   Asquith, *Portrait of Barrie,* 129.

p.116   J. M. Barrie Collection.

p.117   Mackail, *The Story of J. M. B.,* 658.

p.120   Barrie, *The Greenwood Hat,* 26.

Bibliography

Writings of J. M. Barrie

Courage. New York: Charles Scribner's Sons, 1922.

The Greenwood Hat. New York: Charles Scribner's Sons, 1938.

Letters of James M. Barrie. Edited by Viola Meynell. New York: Charles Scribner's Sons, 1947.

The Little White Bird. New York: Charles Scribner's Sons, 1913.

Margaret Ogilvy. New York: Charles Scribner's Sons, 1946.

M'Connachie and J. M. B: Speeches by J. M. Barrie. New York: Charles Scribner's Sons, 1938, 1939.

Papers. The Walter Beinecke Jr. Collection at the Beinecke Rare Book and Manuscript Library, Yale University.

Peter Pan and Wendy. New York: Charles Scribner's Sons, 1928.

Peter Pan in Kensington Gardens. New York: Charles Scribner's Sons, 1906.

Peter Pan: Or the Boy Who Would Not Grow Up. New York: Charles Scribner's Sons, 1928.

Tommy and Grizel. London: Cassell, 1896.

Other Sources

Ansell, Mary. *Dogs and Men*. Salem, NH: Ayer Co. Publishers, 1970.

Asquith, Cynthia. *Portrait of Barrie*. London: James Barrie, 1954.

————. *Diaries 1915-18*. London: Hutchinson and Co., 1968.

Birkin, Andrew. *J. M. Barrie & the Lost Boys: The Love Story that Gave Birth to Peter Pan*. New York: Clarkson N. Potter, 1979.

Dunbar, Janet. *J. M. Barrie: The Man Behind the Image*. Boston: Houghton Mifflin, 1970.

Green, Roger Lancelyn. *Fifty Years of Peter Pan*. London: Peter Davies, 1954.

————. *J. M. Barrie*. New York: Henry Z. Walck, 1961.

Hammerton, J. A. *J. M. Barrie and His Books*. London: Horace Marshall and Son, 1902.

————. *Barrie: The Story of a Genius*. New York: Dodd, Mead, 1929.

————. *Barrieland: A Thrums Pilgrimage*. London: Sampson Low, Marston and Co., 1931.

Hudson, Derek. *Arthur Rackham: His Life and Work*. New York: Charles Scribner's Sons, 1960.

Mackail, Denis. *The Story of J. M. B.* London: Peter Davies, 1941.

Robbins, Phyllis. *Maude Adams: An Intimate Portrait*. New York: Putnam, 1956.

Index

Photo Acknowledgments

The photographs have been reproduced through the courtesy of: p. 1, National Portrait Gallery, London; pp. 2, 43, 78, The Bettmann Archive; pp. 6, 9, 27, 28, 29, 46, 54, 60, 63, 65, 66, 67, 68, 69, 73, 74, 77, 81, 90, 91, 94, 120, The Beinecke Rare Book and Manuscript Library, Yale University; p. 11, Oklahoma State University Theatre, 1989; pp. 12, 14, 34, 106, 115, National Trust for Scotland; pp. 15, 18, 21, 26, 96, 109, J. A. Hammerton, *Barrie: The Story of a Genius* (New York: Dodd, Mead, 1929); pp. 22, 24, 32, 38, 40, 56, Susan Bivin Aller; pp. 45, 100, Illustrated London News; pp. 48, 59, 62, 83, 84, 87 (bottom), 88, 92, 97, 98, 108, 118, © Great Ormond Street Children's Hospital, London; p. 51, J. M. Barrie, *Margaret Ogilvy* (New York: Charles Scribner's Sons, 1946); p. 52, Library of Congress; pp. 55, 117, New York Public Library; p. 70, Courtesy of Mrs. Barbara Edwards, daughter of the artist Arthur Rackham; pp. 72, 105, Stowe-Day Foundation, Hartford, CT; p. 87 (top), Independent Picture Service; pp. 101, 121, The Royal Borough of Kensington and Chelsea, Libraries and Art Service; p. 111, The British Library; p. 112, Bettmann/Hulton.

Front cover portrait courtesy of Library of Congress. Front and back cover illustration by Arthur Rackham, courtesy of University of Liverpool Art Gallery and Collections.

Cover design by Michael Tacheny.